In War Time: A Study of Civil War Era Quilts

In War Time: A Study of Civil War Era Quilts 1850 - 1865

Editors: Dale Drake and Hannah Baughman
Designer: Lisa Erlandson
Photography: Lisa Erlandson

Published By:
American Quilt Study Group
1610 L Street
Lincoln, Nebraska 68508

Dedication
We dedicate this book to all who have experienced the heartache of a loved one away at war. No matter the century, the country or the cause; in times of war, those at home bear a heavy burden.

Acknowledgements

This book is the work of many people who love quilt history. It comes from the efforts of members of the American Quilt Study Group, including the makers of the study quilts as well as the dedicated volunteers who coordinated the project and created this book. Thank you to those of you who give freely of your time and experience to AQSG. Your contributions and support are helping to fulfill the goals of our founders.

A special thank you to AQSG's Judy J. Brott Buss, Executive Director, and Anne E. Schuff, Member Services Coordinator, for all that they do to keep our organization running smoothly.

Contents

Traveling Exhibit Schedule

Please contact the venue for further exhibit information

Monroe County History Center
Bloomington, IN
February to June, 2015

New England Quilt Museum
Lowell, MA
July 1 to October, 2015

Virginia Quilt Museum
Harrisonburg, VA
November, 2015 to March 1, 2016

The Dallas Quilt Show
Dallas, TX
March 11-13, 2016

Quilter's Hall of Fame
Marion, IN
April 1 to July 30, 2016

DeVos Art Museum,
Northern Michigan University
Marquette, MI
September 15 to December 15, 2016

Baldwin Reynolds House Museum
Meadville, PA
December 20, 2016 to February 20,
2017

Gilbert Historical Museum
Gilbert, AZ
March 1 to May 31, 2017

Rocky Mountain Quilt Museum
Golden, CO
June to October 20, 2017

Sheerer Museum of Stillwater
Stillwater, OK
November 1 to February 28, 2018

La Conner Quilt and Textile Museum
La Conner, WA
June 1 to August, 2018

For the latest schedule update, visit
www.americanquiltstudygroup.org

The 2014 AQSG Quilt Study Civil War Quilts

By Lynne Zacek Bassett

The United States in the antebellum and Civil War eras was a much smaller country than it is today. In 1860, the American population was approximately 31 million. Nearly three million men fought in the Civil War, meaning that almost one out of every ten Americans was a soldier or sailor[1]. Every citizen had a relative, friend, or neighbor on the battlefield. With such close connections to the frontlines, women worked heroically at home from 1861 to 1865, to support the war effort and often their families, too, while husbands were away fighting. In the

end, 750,000 men died and tens of thousands more came home with crippling wounds. Thousands of Southerners and those in the border states additionally lost their homes, their incomes and, of course, some also lost their human property. The slaves were freed, but left without a strong support system to assist them in creating a new life. A foretold cataclysm that shifted the nation's history forever, the Civil War affected *all* Americans – soldiers, civilians, men, women, Black, White, Northerner, Southerner, Westerner – and it continues to affect American life and regional antagonisms today.

Textiles touched all lives in the war period. "King Cotton" and the issues surrounding its cultivation and manufacturing – slavery, in particular – were central to the reasons for the war[2]. Textiles clothed and sheltered soldiers and comforted them in hospitals; cotton canvas covered supply wagons and the pontoons of make-do bridges; silk and wool flags symbolized the values of North and South and held the pride and identity of regiments. Quilts sent from home assured soldiers that their sacrifice was honored and their presence was missed, while the families back home could be comforted in the knowledge that they were engaged and helpful to their fighting menfolk. Dustan Walbridge of Peacham, Vermont, encamped with the Union Army outside of Washington, D.C. in 1863, wrote home to his sister: "All last night we had a hard snow and blow storm and it is still snowing we are in our little tents now, and if you could have seen us last night as the snow was swirling around, over and into our little tent, you would have pittied us. but *[sic]* then we didn't suffer. thanks *[sic]* to those quilts that the folks sent us."[3]

[1] http://www.historynet.com/civil-war-soldiers; accessed January 29, 2015. In comparison, today, at the beginning of 2015, the population of the United States stands at more than ten times that number, 325 million, and about one out of 220 Americans serves in the military. http://www.globalfirepower.com/country-military-strength-detail.asp?country_id=United-States-of-America; accessed January 29, 2015.

[2] Madelyn Shaw and Lynne Zacek Bassett, *Homefront & Battlefield: Quilts & Context in the Civil War* (Lowell, MA: American Textile History Museum, 2012), 12–47.

[3] Dustan Walbridge to Ella Watts, 5 April 1863; quoted in Lynn A. Bonfield, "Four Generations of Quilters in One Nineteenth-Century Rural New England Family," in Lynne Z. Bassett, ed., *What's New England About New England Quilts? Proceedings of a Symposium at Old Sturbridge Village June 13, 1998* (Sturbridge, MA: Old Sturbridge Village, 1999), 42.

At home, women expressed their beliefs, fears, strengths, and struggles in their quilts before, during, and after the war. In the debate over slavery in the antebellum period, women sewed quilts and fancy items inked with anti-slavery mottoes to sell at ladies' fairs, to lure the Christmas and New Year's holiday shoppers into awareness and conversation about the controversial subject. A poem written in the center of a cradle quilt sold at a Boston anti-slavery fair in 1836 reads:

Mother! when around your child
You clasp your arms in love,
And when with grateful joy you raise
Your eyes to God above–
Think of the negro-mother,
When her child is torn away–
Sold for a little slave–
Oh then, For that poor mother pray![4]

Concerns over separation encouraged another genre of quilts in the period prior to the war: friendship quilts, in which family members, friends, neighbors, and associates signed pieced calico blocks, often in order to present the finished quilt as a gift to someone who was leaving the community, whether to go west, to go to another parish, or to follow her husband to a new home. Genealogical research on these inscribed quilts often reveals Civil War connections among the names — men who fought, women who lost sons or husbands, and young people who were able to get married only once the war was over.

[4] Cradle quilt attributed to Lydia Maria Child, 1836. Collection of Historic New England, Boston, Massachusetts, 1923-597.

Before and during the war, women pieced, appliquéd, and embroidered quilts as an expression of their patriotism — whether to the United States or to the Confederacy. Quilts bore symbols and mottoes of their firmly held beliefs, including flag imagery, eagles, stars, and phrases such as "Union Forever" and "Rally Round the Flag, Boys!" Another way to express solidarity with their respective cause was to sew quilts for soldiers who were recuperating in hospitals or encamped far from home. While the North was able to organize much of its effort to support Union soldiers and sailors through the U.S. Sanitary Commission, the more rural South labored in smaller groups and individually under difficulties that the North largely escaped. The contribution of Northern and Southern women to the health and comfort of the soldiers was remarkable and necessary to both governments.

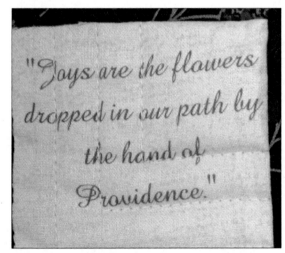

"Joys are the flowers dropped in our path by the hand of Providence."

Although they worked so hard for the soldiers, some women quilted for themselves also, as a diversion from their worries over the lists of dead and wounded that appeared in the newspaper following each battle.

Recognizing the value of a beautiful quilt, soldiers stole them as souvenirs of their war experience or simply because they needed the warmth that a quilt provided. Refugees traded quilts for food, lodging, or other forms of help, and other civilians caught between battling armies hid their quilts with the family silver in the attic or in a hole dug in the yard. Quilts tell many stories of individual, regional, and national struggle in the Civil War.[5]

[5] In addition to Shaw and Bassett, *Homefront & Battlefield*, recommended books on Civil War quilts are: Barbara Brackman, *Quilts from the Civil War* (Lafayette, CA: C & T Publishing, 1997); Barbara Brackman, *Facts & Fabrications: Unraveling the History of Quilts & Slavery* (Lafayette, CA: C & T Publishing, 2006); Bets Ramsay and Merikay Waldvogel, *Southern Quilts: Surviving Relics of the Civil War* (Nashville, TN: Rutledge Hill Press, 1998); and Pam Weeks and Donald Beld, *Civil War Quilts* (Atglen, PA: Schiffer Publishing Co., 2011).

It is only appropriate, then, that in recognition of the Civil War Sesquicentennial, the American Quilt Study Group issued a "Civil War Quilts" challenge. The challenge required participants to identify an inspiration quilt dating from 1850 to 1865. The quilt could be reproduced in whole or in part, or it could be used as the basis for a new meaningful design. Additionally, participants submitted a written statement explaining their motivations and method. Some participants used

the occasion of this challenge to explore the color and design of the period, discovering "a new appreciation for brown, and for the women who made quilts 150 years ago using fabrics of that limited but interesting color palette." Others with ancestral connections to the war grasped the opportunity to research their family history and to interpret it in their quilts: one quilter was inspired to tell the story of her great-grandfather, who had enlisted in the Union Army at the tender age of fourteen.

Women's volunteer work during the war fired the imagination and needles of several participants, who reproduced elements of quilts given to Civil War soldiers by the United States Sanitary Commission or similar soldiers' aid associations. Others were inspired by the patriotic symbolism found in a Civil War era quilt, and carefully stitched the motifs using reproduction fabrics. Antebellum friendship quilts were explored in

some cases, one participant finding that "some of the men on the quilt served in the Civil War and ... some of the women who are unmarried on the quilt married Civil War veterans." Other quilts became tributes to the often uncredited sacrifice of mothers "who have seen their sons off to war:" one participant dedicated her quilt to her great-great-grandmother, who sent two of her sons to serve in the Union Army. Other challenge quilts became metaphors for the political and emotional turmoil of the period, such as "Swirling," a pinwheel design of dark and light colors expressive of the threat to the new republic.

In all, fifty quilts were submitted to the American Quilt Study Group's Civil War Quilt challenge. Twenty-five were chosen to travel in an exhibit. As this book reveals, the challenge was met admirably.

Lynne Zacek Bassett is an independent scholar specializing in New England's historic costume and textiles. She is a recipient of the Costume Society of America's Richard Martin Award for Excellence for her 2004 exhibition and catalog for the Mark Twain House & Museum, *'Modesty Died When Clothes Were Born': Costume in the Life and Literature of Mark Twain.* She and co-author Madelyn Shaw won a bronze medal in history from the Independent Publishers Book Awards for their 2012 publication, *Homefront & Battlefield: Civil War Quilts in Context.* Lynne is also the editor of *Uncoverings,* the annual journal of the American Quilt Study Group. In recognition of her contribution to the field of costume and textile history, the American Antiquarian Society, the Massachusetts Historical Society, Historic New England, and the International Quilt Study Center have elected Lynne to membership in their honorary or advisory societies.

In War Time:
A Study of Civil
War Era Quilts
1850 - 1865

Lucy Belle Clouse
38" x 40"

Joy Swartz
Prescott, Arizona

Lucy Bell Clouse was born in Pennsylvania in March of 1838. She was a teacher in Licking County, Ohio who never married. This inspiration quilt is said to have been made by Lucy after she asked her students to bring bits of fabrics from their mothers, grandmothers, and neighbors. She started the quilt in 1851 and finished it in 1860. At least those are the dates she placed on the quilt, and is confirmed by the family story that came with the quilt. There are many little 'circles' below the vine border that contain fabric added after the quilt was finished - the brown thread shows through to the back. Lucy also put her initials on the quilt and in the last corner added "SPEC," surrounded by quilted hearts. We can only guess at who or what they stand for. Lucy did not use one single piece of white fabric for the background; rather she added rows of white fabric as the quilt grew.

I have found this quilt to be a great resource, as it shows the wonderful variety of fabrics that were available to a quilter in the mid-nineteenth century in northern Ohio. I decided the challenges of this quilt would be - first - to make the quilt using fabric true to the time period. I had a time-appropriate quilt bought many years ago as a "cutter." Most of the fabric for the small quilt came from this old quilt. I was also fortunate enough to have friends give me orphan blocks and bits of fabric from this time frame, plus I had a few of my own. I tried to stay true to her color choices.

Working with old fabric was a bigger challenge than I had anticipated. Some fabrics would simply turn to threads as I appliquéd, and other fabrics disintegrated as I'd brush against them while quilting. Repair

work was necessary once I had finished! I also had to learn how to trapunto to make this quilt. I did more quilting than Lucy did; however, Lucy made this challenging binding on the bias with one inch pieces of fabric. I did not have enough vintage fabric for that luxury.

This quilt took many long hours to complete. I can imagine the quilt was good therapy for Lucy during her evenings alone.

Honoring Civil War Veterans
44" x 44"

Carol W. Gebel
Rocklin, California

I found my inspiration quilt in my own collection. I had purchased it from a dealer in llinois, largely because of two factors: its beautiful mid-nineteenth century fabrics and its names on each block, except for one. This quilt, utilizing the Snowflake block, is a friendship quilt with names. There are no signatures since the names are not inscribed by hand but stamped in ink using individual letters. Each person's name is accompanied by a place name.

I call this quilt the Conklin quilt for the farm in Illinois where the antique dealer purchased the quilt, although the place names on it are in New Hampshire, Vermont, and New York. Genealogical research revealed that some of the men on the quilt served in the Civil War and that some of the women who are unmarried on the quilt married Civil War veterans.

I decided to make a nine block quilt with blocks large enough so I could print the names of these Civil War veterans in the center square of each block. I printed the names by hand. I used reproduction fabrics that reflected the colors and print styles of the Conklin quilt. I hand quilted it using the same simple by-the-piece quilting of the original. As I cut and then joined the piece together, I was reminded that edges cut on the bias can definitely stretch and that when cutting stripes, one needs to consider the placement of the piece in the block to get the stripe's direction to appear as one wants.

Appliqué Quilt, unnamed design, circa 1860. Pioneer Museum of Alabama, Troy, Alabama. Photograph by Mac Holmes.

Louisa's Hope
48" x 48"

Sherry Burkhalter
Newville, Alabama

After presenting a bed turning and lecture at the Troy Pioneer Museum in Troy, Alabama, one quilt on exhibit caught my eye. It was crisp and clean and made of solid color fabrics. It was striking in its simplicity: an unknown appliqué pattern resembling magnolia pods filled with red seeds.

With study I learned that Louisa Anserdena Gibson made the quilt. She was born in 1850, the ninth of sixteen children, in a town called Milo, in Pike County, Alabama. Milo is not found on any current maps, but in 1850 it was a busy town with several stores and a post office. Civil War letters written by

soldiers from Milo were recently discovered in an abandoned house. Louisa's grandparents were some of the early settlers of Milo and Pike County, with one area being called Gibson's Hill.

Louisa was a young teenager when she made the quilt. It is an example of uniform appliqué with amazing precision repeated many times. It was a challenge to replicate such precision and required diligence and perseverance. As I stitched, I pondered what a young girl like Louisa would be feeling as the Civil War raged. I could only imagine that her dreams of courting and marrying a young man were being trampled. Louisa remained unmarried until age thirty-one. The magnolia is emblematic of

the South and I envisioned the pod full of seeds representing her hope of the rebirth of the South after such destruction as came with the war.

Peonies Remembered
42" x 42"

Kathryn Johnson
Charleston, West Virginia

A Peony quilt by M. M. Walker made around 1850 served as the inspiration quilt for this study. The inspiration quilt measures 88" x 90" and is red and green. The quilt center consists of sixteen 12" Peony blocks set on point that alternate with nine 12" appliqué blocks featuring a simple leaf, bud, and blossom. The middle appliqué block is signed by the maker. The border is informal with whimsical finger-trees in two sizes. The batting is thin and the quilting includes feathers, feathered wreathes, and outline quilting with diagonal quilting lines filling open spaces. The quilt is part of my collection. I selected it for study because of the combination of piecing and appliqué techniques, because I have a boundless attraction to red and green quilts, and because I hoped to learn more about the quilt's maker.

In creating the study quilt, I sought to use many elements of the inspiration quilt while staying within the size restrictions. The study quilt center replicates the blocks from the inspiration quilt with four 12" Peony blocks and a single signed appliqué block. Size limitations meant that I could not reproduce the wonderful finger-tree border of the inspiration quilt. A review of other quilts of the period drove my border decisions to include an undulating vine without coordinated corners and with few elements. The appliqué elements (leaves, bud, and blossom) were taken from the inspiration quilt's appliqué block. Unfortunately, the whimsical finger-tree is only present on the quilt's label.

The study quilt is hand pieced, appliquéd, and quilted. While I might have at first romantically thought I was using the same techniques as M. M. Walker, I soon realized that the modern tools and materials I used along with the traditional techniques were making my work much easier. Piecing during a power outage reminded me how easily we take for granted even the light by which we work! I continue to marvel at the inspiration quilt's gracefulness, M. M. Walker's excellent workmanship and the peony's impossibly tiny stem. Unfortunately, I have been unable to unearth more information about M. M. Walker who may have lived in Indiana or Ohio, but hope that a viewer of this study quilt may be able to help in this area.

Lewis' Big Yellow Star
30" x 38"

Susan Craig Spurgeon
Orchard Park, New York

As tempers were unraveling just prior to the Civil War, Lewis Hall Frost (1826 - 1910) and Adaline Lewis Frost (1835 - 1899) were starting their family. First came James W. in 1856 and then Lewis Edson (1858 - 1953). Adaline proved herself a practiced and exacting quilter as she made Bethlehem Star crib quilts for both children.

Lewis' quilt is my inspiration quilt. I wondered if Adaline had chosen the warm two-toned yellow fabric for the star to symbolize a bright guiding light. Or maybe the reason was much simpler. Perhaps that fabric was the only fabric she had in the amount she calculated she would need! The star is impressive. It's beautifully pieced, lies almost flat, and the yellow a nice contrast with the plain white muslin in the star and the Flying Geese. The "sky" fabric, however, was very unattractive! I was intrigued, though. It was likely an overdyed green, originally, and lost its color when exposed to alkaline soaps of the day. Enough of the dyes disappeared so all that remains is a greenish-yellow khaki color and some very small faded blue solid dots in no discernable pattern. Not visible in the Quilt Index photo, dots were clearly

visible when viewing the actual quilt at the New England Quilt Museum! That quilt had obviously been through a lot, so I figured there was a good story in there somewhere.

When planning my study quilt, I decided to adopt the entire quilt design that Adaline drafted and pay homage to that. I approximated the size of the original (30"x 38" vs 36" x 44") but I knew I had to use different fabrics in order to make the quilt really mine. I liked the idea of a yellow star, though. I usually welcome a good challenge so, although not a practiced hand sewer, I attempted to hand piece individual diamonds. I wasn't accurate enough; therefore strip piecing became my method of choice! I did feel that my study quilt deserved to be hand quilted, so I did that ... with trepidation! Adaline's quilting was small, straight, and even. Of interest is that when still a child, Lewis pieced an 87" x 87" quilt of 4-patches set on point. Adaline quilted it later and presented it to him and his bride, Lillian Birdsey (1859-1960).

This was my first quilt study, and what I learned was how to work the process and how to do it differently next time. Of great interest within this research was how 19th century fabric dyes developed.

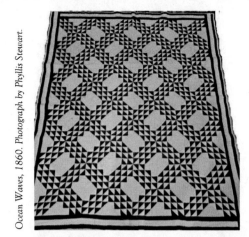

Small Ocean Waves
18" x 22"

Phyllis Stewart
Castle Rock, Colorado

I am blessed to come from a long line of quilt makers. The quilt I chose for the Civil War Quilt study is actually a family quilt, given to me several years ago by my mother, who purchased it from a second cousin for $250. According to family history, the quilt was made by a great-great-great aunt, Presbie Carolyn Smith, who lived in Missouri. The quilt is made of only two fabrics which surprises me a bit – that means she had enough money to buy some yardage rather than make a quilt from scraps. As the family history goes, the thread is unusually thick because it was hand-spun by slaves.

The quilt was beautifully and precisely pieced and quilted, a difficult feat for me to accomplish in miniature. I chose to try and replicate it as accurately as possible, but shrinking the block size from 1 ⅞" down to ¼" made it a challenge. I couldn't help but wonder how it was for Presbie, making this quilt by hand with some kind of template and sewing by kerosene light. It made me more thankful for my modern tools, including the sewing machine. I was even able to redesign the quilt in EQ7 – wouldn't she have been shocked at how we make quilts today?

About 20 years ago my aunt compiled a number of pioneer stories about my grandmother (Mary Hurchel Bourgain, 1897-1974) and her life; although this is not a story about Presbie, it is about the Civil War era, and the impact it had on our country and quilters:

"While still in Missouri, Mary Hurchel often visited her Grandmother Dobyns to the delight of both of them. One hot day when her grandmother was sweeping the wide front porch, she stopped suddenly at the sight of a man walking down the dusty road. They stared at each other from a distance but no sign was given nor word spoken. After the lonely figure was out of sight, her grandmother told Mary Hurchel the he was her

(Grandmother Dobyns) brother. During the Civil War the Connell family was on the Union side except this one brother; he had mortgaged his land and given the money to the Confederate cause. All was lost, of course, and his part of the family was penniless. Other brothers fought with the Union Army and the family never became reconciled as a unit again."

Union
34" x 44"

Kay Ross
Long Beach, California

This quilt immediately spoke to me. It is visually and symbolically a statement of national patriotism, commitment, and pride. This is evident from the quilt's flags, shield, and word "unity." The twenty baskets are filled with a variety of flowers and berries symbolizing hope, peace, and beauty for all. This message has continued through the decades and still resonates with our nation today and has definitely had an impact on me.

Martha McFeely used solid red, green, and orange fabrics and quilted it using wreaths, outlines, and crosshatching, which are representative of mid-nineteenth century quilts. My desire was to reproduce this quilt, staying as true as possible to the maker's creative inspiration.

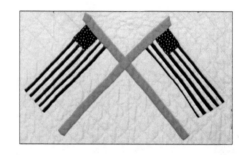

The progress of this project became a shared interest for family, neighbors, and a dear friend. Moreover, it advanced my quilting skills, patience, and perseverance, giving me a great sense of accomplishment.

A surprising aspect of the project was that upon studying Martha McFeely's quilt and learning about her life, I felt a connection to her. The Indiana Historical Society has fifty letters written to her by her beau, Benjamin Fry, while he served four years in the Civil War. These letters told of his daily routines, schedules, marches, battles, and raids. When he wrote about Martha McFeely, he called her Mattie. The letters mentioned Mattie teaching, going to school, raising money for a community flag, and sending supplies to the soldiers. On March 10, 1863, Benjamin bought a gold pen for Mattie and wrote "... as a remembrance of one that has left home to defend his country and to defend your peaceable firesides so that one and all may enjoy life and liberty" (Fry Family Letters, 1863. Indiana Historical Society). I like to think that Martha McFeely used fabric and stitches to commemorate Benjamin Fry's commitment and sacrifices for his country.

Reproducing this quilt, reading the war letters, and learning about Martha and Benjamin Fry have made this quilt a significant historical treasure for me. The quilt's symbolism echoes the thoughts and lives of the American soldiers.

I feel humbled and reverent to have had this opportunity to participate in this study project. Thank you to the Indiana State Museum and the Indiana Historical Society for their support, encouragement, and assistance.

Gunboat Quilt by Martha Jane Dixon Hatter, circa 1861. Collection of the Birmingham Museum of Art; purchased with partial funds from The Quilt Conservancy, 1954.209. Photograph by Sean Pathasema.

Petticoat Quilt
31" x 32"

Ann R. Walls
Virginia Beach, Virginia

Since I have lived in the South most of my life, I thought it would be appropriate to study quilts made by Southern women. Gunboat Quilts caught my attention right away. I envisioned myself in the position of a Southern woman – it was early in the war. The blockades were established but supplies were still available. I wanted to do anything I could to bring our men home. The call went out to provide quilts for auction to raise funds to purchase gun boats and I answered the call.

The Alabama Gunboat Quilt by Martha Hatter is one of the few quilts that we can definitively trace to these auctions. It is an especially intricate and lovely example of craftsmanship which includes beading and embroidery. The vase on my quilt is from Judy Ann Breneman's instructions for a Confederate Gunboat Quilt. For the bouquet, I thought I would simply find a bouquet of flowers in a fabric, cut it out, and appliqué it to the center block. My research quickly dispelled that notion. Barbara Brackman explained American women cut floral chintz flowers and then rearranged them.

Jane's quilt was completely by hand. I used my machine as much as possible. The butterfly is an especially modern method. I found a butterfly image of the right size on a graduation card, scanned it, printed the butterfly on fabric, and attached it by thread, painting the black wings. The quilting was another matter. I used the bar attached to my even feed foot to space the lines in the center crosshatching. This went well until my fourth turn back into my starting point. The lines didn't come together in the perfection shown by Jane's quilt. In this case, the marking of chalk lines would have been a better option. It still looks okay from a galloping horse, but I know it's there.

I learned that although things change, they also remain the same. Modern methods are great, but then again, the old methods work just as well and sometimes better than new, supposedly improved methods. A quilter decides on her methods by what gives her the most joy.

Jill's Friendship Album Star

49" x 49"

Jill Meszaros
Cambridge Springs, Pennsylvania

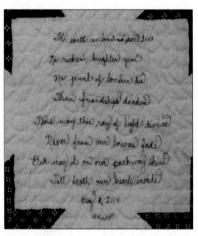

Friendship Album Star, 1858. Crawford County Historical Society. Photograph by Paige Pilewski.

I believe my study quilt chose me. The "Friendship Album Star" is an 88" x 88" blue and white signature quilt, with a nearly-identical twin belonging to the Crawford County Historical Society in Meadville, Pennsylvania. Both were signed by women in the Meadville area and inscribed with the same poem. They date from the Quilt Study time period of 1850-1865 and either would have been an appropriate choice. When I realized the Blue / White Album Star was dated May 8, I was convinced it needed to be my study quilt. You see, I was born on May 8. A connection between the past and present was in the making ... and little did I know it at the time, but an inaccuracy was about to be corrected.

With my personal connection to the date of the quilt, I decided to replicate the original design in every way possible. I drafted my own block pattern. I began with a LeMoyne Star block, and modified it to create cut-off diamonds and an octagon shape for the center. The center octagon shape and reducing the block were a challenge to say the least. Then, finding a blue and white print fabric, in the appropriate scale, became a six-week search. With those challenges out of the way, I could enjoy the piecing and quilting. I hand pieced 49 blocks, the same unsymmetrical sawtooth border and asked for signatures from my family and friends. I also hand quilted identical designs of a double wreath and close diagonal lines.

Then something unexpected occurred: upon closer examination of the quilt I found several blocks clearly inscribed with the year 1858; however, the documented year was 1855. Someone had misread 1858 for 1855. Family tradition related the quilt being made for an "Aunt Nellie," born 1858, died 1886. However with the misreading of the year, that was thought to be inaccurate, so another story was created. I believe we can now go back to the original family provenance of the quilt, it being made for Nellie born in 1858. The twin to this quilt is interestingly dated April 1858. (More research will follow.)

I feel like Nellie drew me to this quilt. She wanted the date and the family provenance restored. This is why I decided to inscribe my quilt with the same poem as the two twin star quilts, making the connection of past and present complete.

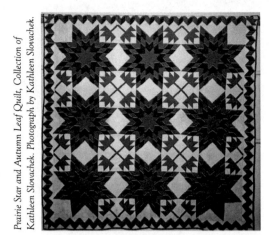

Prairie Star and Maple Leaves
42" x 42"

Carol Butzke
Mequon, Wisconsin

Since the 2014 AQSG Seminar is being held in Wisconsin, I was focused on studying a quilt that was a part of *Wisconsin Quilts, Stories in Stitches*, the state's published quilt history project book. In perusing the book, I found exactly what I wanted – a red, white and green quilt with the dates of 1860-1865. What was even more exciting, the quilt had been owned by a mentor of mine for NQA certification for quilt judging, Geneva Watts of Racine, Wisconsin, and her son, Rodney. Geneva made her mark as an appliqué artist, teacher, and much more. Geneva has passed away since the publication of the book, but I was able to contact her daughter and daughter-in-law. Kathleen, the daughter-in-law, who has the quilt in her possession, was most gracious in giving permission to use the quilt for study, and provided me with the necessary photos. Thus, my quilt is a tribute to Geneva.

The original maker of the quilt was Mary Strove Ellis (1845-1937). It became her wedding quilt. It has remained in the family through the generations.

I do not know the block sizes of the original quilt, but have drafted them to 18" blocks. A good experience to revisit, since I had not drafted quilt blocks in a number of years.

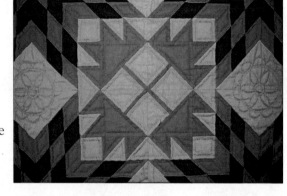

One of the events for AQSG in Milwaukee is an exhibit of quilts with antimony orange/chrome orange, also known as "cheddar." I have spent a considerable amount of time researching orange dyes and their timeline. The mineral orange dyes were available in the years of the Civil War and thus, it was natural to use them in this interpretation. For me, there is a strong connection to Wisconsin in this piece: Geneva Watts and her contribution to Wisconsin quilters, "America's Dairyland," the beauty of Wisconsin's autumn, and of course, the Green Bay Packers.

So Geneva, this one is for you and how you have inspired my career.

All Hands Around Quilt, 1864. Minnesota Historical Society Collections.

Remembering the First Minnesota

30" x 30"

Jonda DeLozier
Bloomington, Minnesota

When I realized the 2014 Quilt Study was going to be on the Civil War, I decided my home state of Minnesota would be my "jumping-off point." The Civil War exhibit at the Minnesota History Center was right in front of me! On display was a beautiful red, white, and blue star quilt, dated 1864, made by Emelina Bistodeau and five other unnamed women.

After visiting the exhibit, I was able to photograph the quilts in the History Center's archives. What an unexpected treat! Actually touching Emelina's quilt and helping to unroll it was quite a different experience than seeing it through a display case. Viewing the workmanship, piecing, and quilting was quite humbling; and to think, this incredible quilt was made during the Civil War. The star design and choice of colors seemed appropriate for the time.

Emelina's quilt design, All Hands Around, consists of LeMoyne Stars. Originally I had planned to duplicate the quilt in miniature, but creating even the first block was a challenge for me! After a few unsuccessful attempts at making the blocks without "modern conveniences," I discovered a wonderful LeMoyne Star ruler. But even with my stars looking better, I decided to make a simplified version of the original. I now see Emelina's quilt as beautiful in its "simplicity."

While cutting my blocks I realized I had different qualities of fabrics and was a bit upset thinking my blocks wouldn't be consistent. I finally asked myself, "What did our ancestors have available to them?" Early quilters had neither an unlimited fabric selection nor convenient tools, but their quilts are as beautiful as any created today.

While reading some of our history, I discovered Minnesota was the first state to respond to President Lincoln's request for volunteer regiments; 25,000 men, or about half our eligible male population, left their homes to serve. The First Minnesota Volunteer Infantry Division mustered in in April of 1861 and

marched from Ft. Snelling to St. Anthony in May. I have dedicated my quilt to the memory of those who served in the First Minnesota.

Who knows – perhaps Emelina, who lived in St. Anthony, was there to support these courageous men when they left their families, and maybe she had them in mind when she made her star quilt.

31

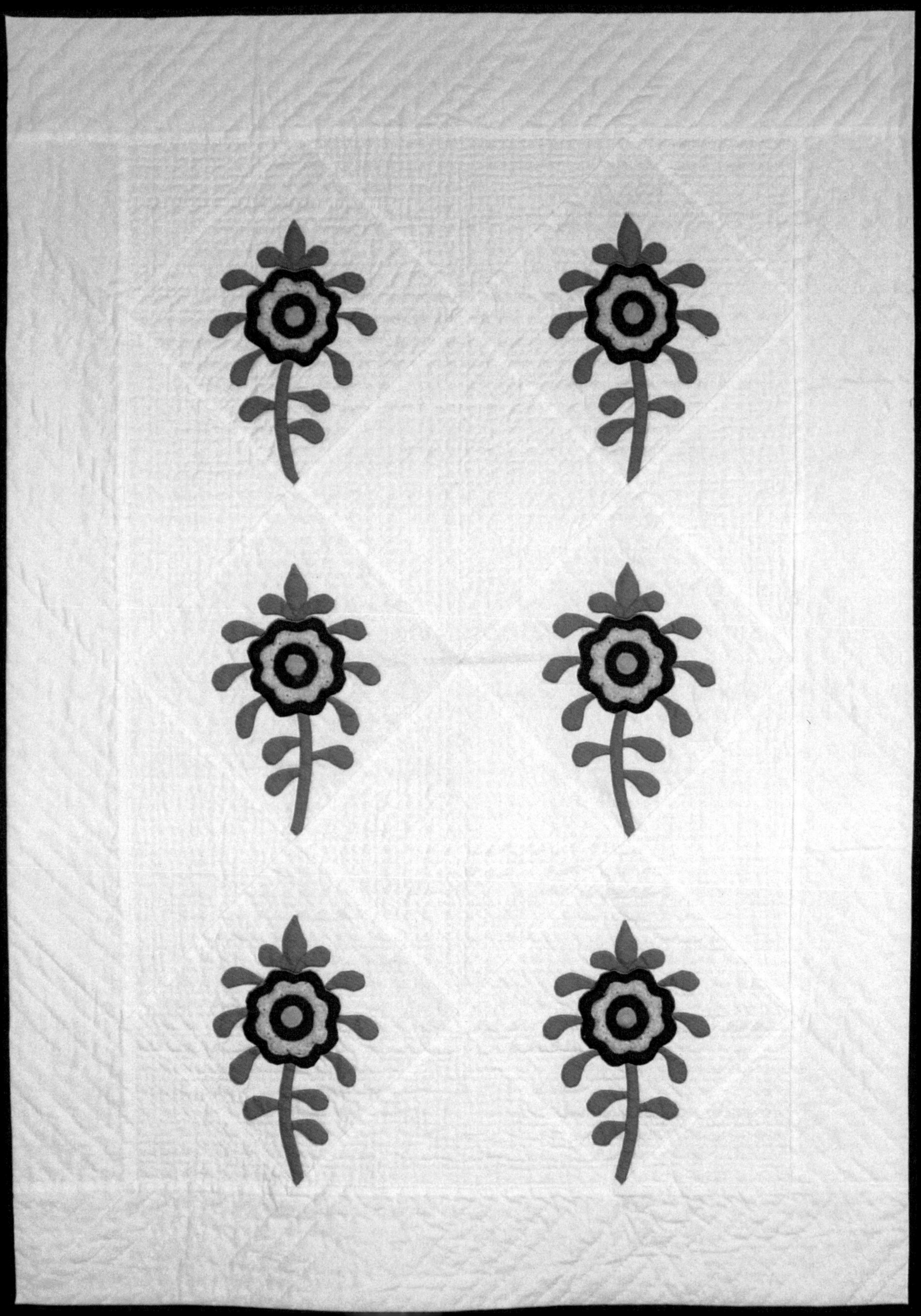

Rose of Sharon
35" x 46"

Carol C. Wheelock
Waitsfield, Vermont

I've always loved the Civil War-era red and green appliquéd quilts, so it was natural for me to choose one as my inspiration quilt. The fact that I had never appliquéd, hand quilted, or done any trapunto before didn't deter me, although in retrospect, it probably should have.

My inspiration quilt resides at the Sheldon Museum in Middlebury, Vermont. It was made by Samantha Holbrook, a young woman who was born in Hyde Park, Vermont, in 1837. I could find out very little about Samantha, other than the fact that she married Emerson B. Reed, a joiner and woodworker who operated a planing mill and job shop in Cady's Falls, Vermont, a town which was, and remains, a wide spot in the road. She and Emerson lived in nearby Morristown, where they also ran a farm. Her marriage to Emerson was after the 1860 census. This quilt could easily have been made for her wedding. And it must have been saved for special occasions, as it does not appear to have been used that much. Records indicate that Samantha had only one (living) child, a daughter Effie, who was born in 1869. Effie passed this wonderful quilt down to her daughter, who donated it to the Sheldon Museum in Middlebury.

I was attracted to Samantha's folk art version of the Rose of Sharon block. Samantha's quilt is delightfully simple yet deceptively complex, especially when one considers the lack of measuring and cutting tools at the time. She even used trapunto to give the quilt a greater sense of depth. Samantha appears to have assembled the on-point blocks potholder style.

Since I collect crib (and doll) quilts, I chose to make a crib or cradle quilt version that could have been a companion to Samantha's original full-size quilt. With the help of a modern copier, I reduced the size of the blocks by 50% and greatly simplified the border to create this mini version. I limited the trapunto to pieces large enough to make it possible for me to do. I like to think Samantha would have appreciated it for her daughter.

Surya Dragon Rising
42" x 42"

Christine Turner
DuPont, Washington

I have always been drawn to the "pointy" quilts, so when this challenge was announced, I first searched the Quilt Index for ideas, but then approached the one person who I knew had an extensive collection of "pointy"-patterned quilts. Bill Volckening was game to help me out, and sent me

pictures of three quilts in his collection that fit the time frame.

I chose this one and began the design process by figuring the reduction from the original size of 84" x 84" to the allowed 50" x 50" size, and then doing the designing in my Electric Quilt 7 software. I had planned to replicate the entire quilt, but an injury to my left arm cut several months off my sewing schedule, forcing me to make the decision to not do the half-blocks around the left side and bottom of the original quilt.

Unlike the original quilter, I had technology to help with the design and pattern printing, and equipment such as rotary cutters, rulers, and special foundation-piecing paper to help with accurate sewing. Without those tools, I wouldn't have dared tackle this pattern. The whole process of doing this challenge reinforced my absolute respect and admiration for any quilter taking on this design, no matter the time period.

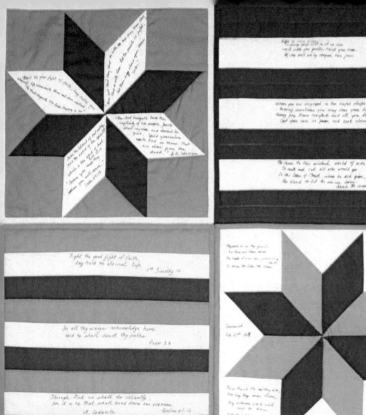
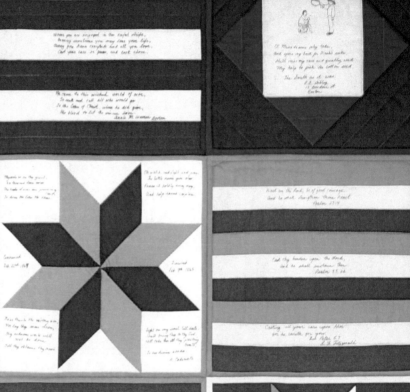

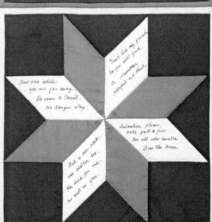

Civil War Central Medallion Quilt, 1865. Collection of the New England Quilt Museum. Photograph by David Stansbury.

A Quilt for a Civil War Soldier

37" x 37"

Laura Lane
Marlborough, Massachussetts

During the Civil War, groups of women from both the North and South knitted and sewed mittens, socks, shirts, quilts, and other items needed by their soldiers. My inspiration quilt was made by a group of at least seven women in and around Boston, Massachusetts. The completion date of the quilt is inscribed on the central star block: February 9, 1865. The quilt was given to James George serving in the New York Infantry. George had seen action in the battles at Gettysburg and Fredericksburg, and was captured at the Battle of the Wilderness. After six months in the infamous Andersonville Prison, George was paroled and spent time in a Washington, DC hospital recuperating before his discharge in June, 1865. He probably received the quilt while in the hospital. The quilt was treasured and passed down through several generations of James George's family along with letters written by George on the battlefield, military documents, and a chess set carved from rat bones while George was in Andersonville Prison. James George died in 1871, his health affected by his imprisonment.

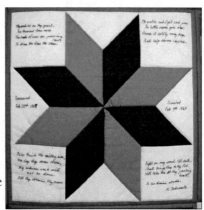

I first saw James George's quilt in 2004, the day a descendant donated it to the New England Quilt Museum. I was drawn to the many inscriptions and ink drawings on the blocks. The inscriptions include many Bible verses, anti-slavery sentiments, and inspirational verses of poetry. Perhaps these written messages also inspired James George's descendants to keep and treasure the quilt, even though it was worn. Many blocks are signed by the makers and some contain addresses. I have chosen to replicate the nine blocks of the quilt's central medallion at their original size of twelve inches square. I transcribed the inscriptions on these blocks and inscribed them on the blocks of my quilt. The inscriptions on one block were unreadable due to fabric loss, so I used inscriptions from another block in the quilt.

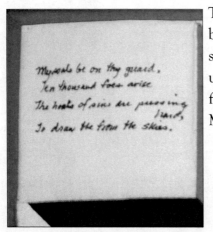

The thirty-five blocks of the original quilt are individually quilted and bound, a technique found on many of the few surviving Civil War soldier quilts. I have made my blocks "pot-holder style," an expression used by quilt historian Pam Weeks to describe this technique. The fabric used on the backs of my blocks is from a 2012 line of fabric from Marcus Fabrics called *Union Forever* based on my inspiration quilt.

Dancing Path
48" x 48"

Nancy Ostman
Gordon, New York

Maze Quilt, The Daughters of the American Revolution Museum, Washington DC. Gift of Margaret Willis. Photograph by Mark Gulezian.

The geometry of Margaret Cabell McClelland's quilt captivated me. I had wanted to make a red and white quilt since the 2011 New York City exhibit, "Infinite Variety." Labyrinths in quilts, stone, corn, and snow are popular today, but finding one in an 1850s quilt surprised me. It was an easy choice, but not an easy quilt.

Margaret created an original maze, or puzzle with pathway choices. I became lost when I tried to reproduce her maze. I chose a more symmetrical labyrinth. When I examined a Hmong appliqué, I realized the technique suited my purpose.

Margaret's maze purportedly was based on the labyrinth floor of French Amiens Cathedral. The original floor, dating from 1288, was torn out in 1827, but replicated in the 1890s. The center stone documents in poetry the date of the cathedral's beginning and completion, names three architects, acknowledges the bishop who commissioned it, and notes Louis IX was King. The quilt reflects the Greek Revival style popular in the USA from 1820 to 1850. Greek designs were used to indicate pride in independence and democracy. Garden mazes were part of the era's landscape design. Margaret's childhood home in Virginia had a boxwood maze.

I learned about labyrinths as I examined her quilt motifs. Instead of Margaret's Greek key, I used a meander on the border. A meander forms a labyrinth by lining units up, arranging them on a grid, or by stacking units and then stretching them around like silly putty until the sides meet in the center. The corner motifs or "seeds" reminded me of old stone forts. If four are set back to back against a cross, the points can be connected cleverly to draw a simple labyrinth. Such labyrinths are distributed around the world.

Labyrinths were said to form protective walls around ancient cities. The hexagons on Margaret's quilt represent fortification locations where invaders were vulnerable as they rounded a sharp corner. Likewise, the crenellations on her strip border marked fortifications. Margaret may have been well versed in military history; her great-grandfather, grandfather, father, and son had military careers.

Labyrinths also are used in processions and dances. For instance, a traditional Latvian dance has participants join hands in a long line to follow a leader in an elaborate circular path that enables dancers to greet everyone else as they pass. The "Dancing Path" simulates a Baltic labyrinth.

39

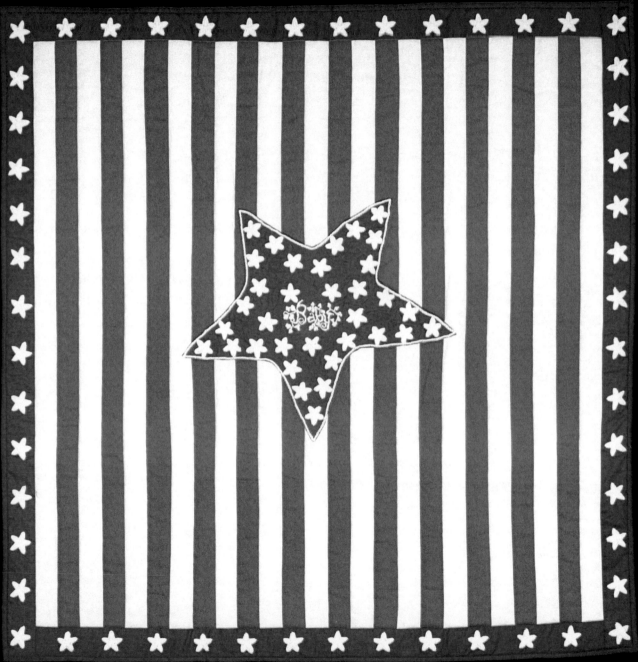

My Baby
36" x 36"

Pamela Roberts Lindsay
Santa Paula, California

I selected "The Patriotic Crib Quilt" from the American Folk Art Museum (1978.42.1) because it captured my imagination from the moment I first saw it in a photograph in Sandi Fox's book, *Small Endearments: Nineteenth-Century Quilts for Children.*

This quilt presented so many questions, I eventually came to the realization that I would never know anything beyond the museum's label for the quilt: "Artist unidentified, possibly Kansas, 1861 – 1875, cotton with cotton embroidery, 36 ¾ x 36 inches, gift of Phyllis Haders."

I was fortunate to have Lauren Arnold from the American Folk Art Museum go to storage and take additional close-up photographs for me. These photographs allowed me to examine the quilt more closely.

Peterson's Magazine published a color illustration in July 1861 titled, *The Stars and Stripes Bed-Quilt.* This illustration features red and white stripes, a blue border with thirty stars and a square center medallion containing thirty-four stars.

Assuming my quiltmaker was inspired by the illustration, her interpretation was to embroider fifty-two stars in the borders, construct the center as a star, and embroider thirty-four smaller stars in the large center star.

The August 1861 installment of *Peterson's Magazine* has a page titled, "Varieties in Embroidery." The word "Baby" embroidered on the center panel of the quilt matches the style, motif, and wording in the illustration.

I chose to make a replica of the quilt, due to its small size. The original quilt was made from homespun and home-dyed fabric, quilted simply. The back is printed in a foulard style with pink and red flowers. The edge is finished with a straight of grain binding turned front to back.

I am very grateful for the assistance provided by Lauren Arnold of the American Folk Art Museum. The process of asking for permission from the museum initially intimidated me. The assistance and encouragement provided by the museum made this a very positive experience.

I recognize the importance of documenting quilts for future reference. Gathering the information of who, what, why, and where quilts are made is important to the context of quiltmaking as an art and social commentary. Quilts have stories to tell and it is important to preserve the quilts and the stories they tell. I will never know the who, what, why, and where of my study quilt, but I will do my best to document my quilts.

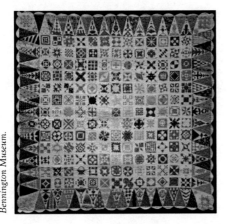

Civil War Sampler
36" x 44"

Catherine Noll Litwinow
Bettendorf, Iowa

I used the Jane A. Stickle Quilt as my inspiration quilt. When my parents saw the Stickle quilt at the Bennington Vermont Museum they both thought the quilt magnificent! I then purchased *Dear Jane: The Two Hundred Twenty-five Patterns from the 1863 Jane A. Stickle Quilt* by Brenda Manges Papadakis. Brenda says that Jane was born on April 8, 1817, the daughter of Erastus Blakely and Sarah Rein. "Jane's marriage to Walter A. Stickle is presumed from the census of 1850 ... it does not appear that Jane and Walter had children of their own." Brenda does not mention if Walter served in the Civil War. He was not included on a list of Vermont Civil War veterans.

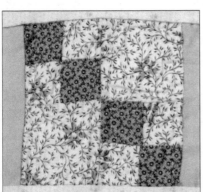

I have been collecting Civil War reproduction fabrics forever. My original plan was to make the quilt a true sampler, with no repeated fabric or pattern. But it just became too much fun hand stitching the blocks using the same pattern in the different color ways! I did use several patterns from the Stickle quilt and several Carol Doak paper foundation patterns. I drafted many of the patterns. Some of the fabric lines I used were: Metropolitan Fair, Conestoga, Charleston, Jo's Calicos, Civil War Crossings, Sturbridge Village, Along the Fence, Lancaster, Anna's Starry Night, Fredericksburg, Carriage House, 1840 Birds and Basics, Gingham Rose, and Material Pleasures.

For my study quilt I have incorporated many double pink fabrics. The barn raising setting appealed to me. I started with a double pink in the center. The following rows were stitched with beige, blue, pink, and green fabrics. I ended the corner sections with beiges and finished with double pink corners. The double pink diamond of blocks just sparkle. The backing is a Judie Rothermel Charleston fabric.

I feel I have a connection with Jane. Her maiden name was Blakely. My father's mother's maiden name was Bleakly. So there could be a possibility that, somewhere in the past, someone switched the "e" between Bleakly and Blakely. And I have always felt that Judie Rothermel's husband and I could be cousins. My great-great-grandmother was Barbara Rothermel Noll. So I consider Judie to be a cousin.

43

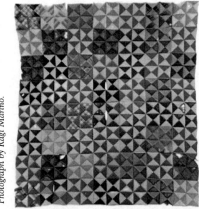

A Soldier's Blanket - Revisited

38" x 45"

Rägi Marino
Cedar Hill, Texas

When the 2014 AQSG Quilt Study "Civil War Quilts: 1850 - 1865" was announced, I knew I would have to look beyond the quilts I owned or could readily access. Not knowing where else to start, I went through the list of museums in the greater Dallas Fort Worth area, noting those that included the Civil War era. To my surprise I discovered the Texas Civil War Museum in Fort Worth. The museum includes both Union and Confederate artifacts, and to my delight several quilts which are owned by the Texas Division United Daughters of the Confederacy.

One quilt in particular caught my attention: "A Soldier's Blanket." This belonged to Lieutenant Jesse Russell Youree of Company E 34th Texas Cavalry at Bonham, Texas. Serving in the Trans-Mississippi Army, he was captured at the Battle of Yellow Bayou and spent time in a Union prison prior to returning to his regiment. Lt. Youree carried this quilt during the war. According to family tradition, this was the replacement quilt for an earlier one which had been put under cannon wheels to help pull them from the mud.

"A Soldier's Blanket" measures 53" x 60" and consists of 56 approximately 7½" x 7½" "blocks." It was made using wool fabrics, including numerous pieces of what appear to be two different "butternut" Confederate uniform fabrics. The quilt is entirely sewn by hand, apparently by more than one person as the stitches are not uniform. The quilt is constructed using an unusual "quilt-as-you-go" method, with squares of fabric folded in half to form triangles, stuffed with cotton and whip-stitched together. Each unit consists of four squares of fabrics, and the blocks consist of four units sewn together into a pattern referred to as "Broken Dishes," "A Simple Quilt Block," and "The Double Square" in Barbara Brackman's *Encyclopedia of Pieced Quilt Patterns*, although this quilt predates any of the references given.

I was inspired to draw a design using a different, more organized color scheme than the original scrappy quilt: "butternut," gray, and blue of the Civil War-era uniforms, with red and gold accents as appeared on some of the officers' uniforms.

45

Civil War Soldiers Study Quilt
45" x 45"

Nancy Bavor
Los Altos Hill, California

When I first saw this quilt, I was stunned by its ambitiousness, the technical challenge it presented to the maker and the wide range of fabrics. I was also intrigued with its imagery of women, soldiers marching and on horseback, and especially, the story connected with it. The early quilt historian Florence Peto described the quilt in her 1949 book *American Quilts and Coverlets* and sold it to the Shelburne Museum in 1952. According to Peto, a Union soldier made this medallion quilt while recovering from his wounds. Images of soldiers are depicted alongside hearts, birds, plants, and moons. The female silhouettes in the center are based on a trademark figure adopted in 1780 by the manufacturer of Baker's Chocolate, which had been copied from Jean-Etienne Liotard's earlier pastel, *La Belle Chocolatiere*.

My version of "Civil War Soldiers" is a scaled down reproduction of the original. However, I resolved to construct it using as many 20th and 21st century quilt making techniques as possible. I used a digital projector to project an image of the original onto graph paper, reduced it to meet the AQSG Study Quilt size requirements, and traced the basic layout and appliqué figures. I bought fabrics at quilt stores, festivals, and online. I used a rotary cutter to cut all the angular shapes, fusible web to fuse the figures to the background, basting spray to hold it together for quilting, and a simulated hand-quilting stitch on my 21st century sewing machine to quilt it.

While working on this project, I imagined what it might have been like to be a recovering soldier, with leisure time to sit and sew but still haunted by images of war. I fantasized that his days were less frantic than mine. Even using modern methods this project took a long time to complete, and by the time I reached the outer border I ran out of steam. Two borders of the original incorporate triangles and squares that are a much larger scale than the rest of the quilt; perhaps the maker had the same "ready to be done" feeling that I did. Perhaps he had recovered enough to go home.

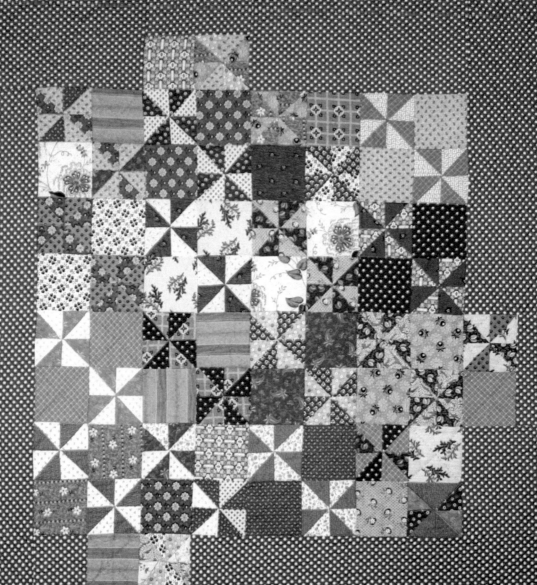

Swirling
36" x 36"

Marjorie J. Farquharson
Needham, Massachusetts

When I made my selection for the AQSG Quilt Study of Civil War era quilts, I felt that this particular piece represented that time period for me. One can only imagine the turmoil in the country and among families during the 1860s. The quilt suggested that to me with the dark colors and simple pattern. Despite that, the unknown quilter's work has lighter areas with color and movement within the design. Her quilt reflects a sophisticated simplicity. Perhaps as the quilter was piecing it during the actual war years, she was hoping for the conclusion to the conflict that so divided our country. Was she longing for a husband, son, father, or brother who was fighting in the war? One wonders whether this quilt was made early in the maker's years of quilt construction or later. Did she previously appliqué flowers in brighter or lighter colors? Would she continue making quilts that were pieced with more subdued colors after the war years?

When I made my quilt, I thought of all of the events and ideas that were swirling around and threatening to break our new democracy. Some of my blocks extend into the borders to represent the fissure in our country.

My inspiration quilt is cataloged by the International Quilt Study Center as circa 1865. It was hand pieced, the quilting stitches are 6 to 7 to an inch, and there is no inscription. As we celebrate the Sesquicentennial of the Civil War, the quilt represents a metaphor for our country. This quilt still exists after all of these years just as the United States survived the conflict.

49

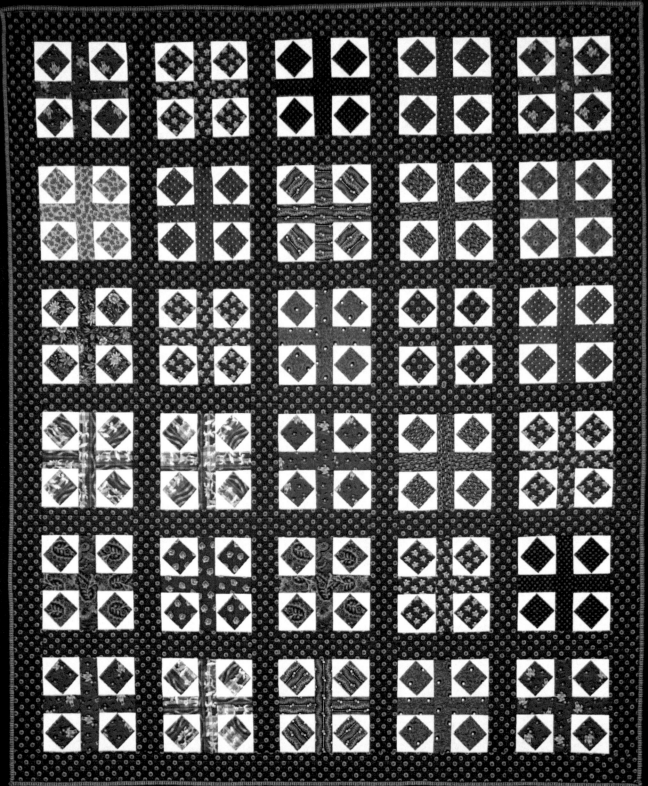

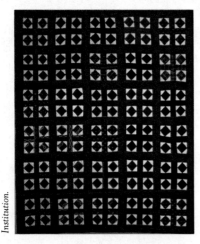

Celia Corwin's "Economy" Pieced Quilt, 1860-1865, National Museum of American History, Smithsonian Institution.

Celia Corwin's "Economy" Variation
40" x 34"

Anita Loscalzo
Dover, Massachusetts

In searching for an inspiration quilt from the Civil War years, I was struck by the use of mostly subdued madder textiles in the quilt made by Celia Corwin of Orange County, New York, between 1860 and 1865 in the collection of the Smithsonian Institution's National Museum of American History (TE*T07119). Her use of fabrics and layout differ greatly with another Economy block pieced quilt made in New Jersey between 1840 and 1850 that I greatly admire in the collection of the Burlington County (New Jersey) Historical Society (BHS x800.20). The Burlington quilt is composed of a wide variety of bright dress prints (particularly those colored with Prussian blue) popular at the time of its making. The contrasting palettes of the two quilts mirror the change in taste for dress goods from the mid-1840s to the late 1850s in the United States.

Celia's "Economy" blocks are a simplification of a true Economy block, eliminating the outer enclosing squares, in effect becoming Squares-Within-Squares. She has then set them in groups of four separated by a cross of the same fabric. In turn, each group of four is separated from one another by a polka-dot sashing, set in six rows of five block sets. Four blocks of matching fabric are carefully placed in the corners, while the rest of the blocks are randomly placed. The Burlington quilt's true Economy blocks are set on point in thirteen rows of thirteen blocks side-by-side alternating with twelve rows of twelve plain muslin blocks set on point, giving the quilt a checkerboard effect.

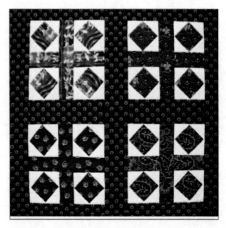

While I was able to retain the spirit of the original in most of my fabric selections, I was unable to find or reproduce an appropriate pentagraph outlined polka-dot print in the madder palette for the sashings (such fabrics were produced around 1855). I found this quite frustrating, because I own a circa 1855 quilt with the exact fabric in its sashings.

I chose to replicate Celia's block design and layout, but adapted it for paper-piecing by machine instead of hand-piecing. Celia added a good deal of hand quilting by using parallel lines in the vertical sashings and concentric diamonds in the squares' areas that spill into the horizontal and outer sashings. I have greatly simplified the quilting and instead accomplished it by machine. Would Celia have made her piece by machine if given the opportunity or, perhaps, owning a sewing machine, did she make the conscious decision to use hand techniques only?

51

Red and Green Pomegranate Quilt, collection of
Deanna M. Velie. Photograph by Deanna M. Velie.

Le Petite Pomegranate
47" x 43"

Deanna M. Velie
Longmont, Colorado

My heart skips a beat when I see a red and green quilt. Pieced or appliquéd, it doesn't matter. I want to make them all. But then isn't that how all quiltmakers feel when they see a quilt they love?

When I saw this red and green pomegranate quilt hanging in a flea market I instantly fell in love! No matter that the red fabrics were shattering and faded and that there were stains and tears, I had to have it. I knew it would make the perfect skirt underneath our Christmas tree.

I was encouraged by my fellow quilt historians to reproduce the quilt for the 2014 Civil War Quilt Study. I have never entered a quilt study or quilt contest before, but I was up for the challenge!

I reduced the pattern by exactly one half. After careful measurement, I realized I could reproduce the quilt in its entirety. The original quilt had been trimmed around all four sides. You will notice from the picture there are random pomegranates along the sides. It also looks as though there was a red border attached at one point. I do not know if other pomegranates were appliquéd on this border or how large the border would have been. I chose to eliminate these pomegranates and make a more symmetrically designed quilt.

It became apparent when studying the construction of this quilt that perhaps more than one person was involved in the construction of the pomegranates, or the maker was unsure of the best way to complete

the pomegranates. I too found there was no right or wrong way to stitch them together.

This pomegranate quilt was quite a challenge to construct. I had originally planned to reproduce the quilt in its original full size. But after making "La Petite Pomegranate," I am quite satisfied with the smaller version.

Walter C. Veazie
37" x 37"

Anne Sonner
Walnut, California

My study quilt was inspired by Stella Rubin's "Central Medallion Quilt: Circa 1860; Pennsylvania." I like this quilt's combination of orderly pieced blocks surrounding a center of exuberant appliquéd flowers.

It inspired me to tell the story of my great-grandfather, Walter C. Veazie. Walter enlisted in the Union Army shortly before his fifteenth birthday and served for three years during the Civil War. According to my father, Walter never talked about the war because it was "too terrible."

Young Walter is depicted in the center of my quilt, wearing his uniform and standing under an elm tree in his hometown of Randolph, Massachusetts. Symbols in the background hint at his later life, including his marriage, work as a minister, and his lifelong interest in stamp collecting.

Walter overcame many obstacles during his remarkable life. His mother died when he was five. He quit school as a boy to help support the family. After the war, he led an oxen train across the country, mined for gold in Montana Territory, and worked as a carpenter. The last 50 years of his life he dedicated to the Christian ministry. Although Walter had little formal education, he learned Greek and was a critical reader and deep thinker.

In designing my study quilt, I changed the checkerboard blocks of the inspiration quilt to album blocks, and inscribed them with the names of Walter's relatives, starting with his parents and ending with my sons. The flowers on my quilt are the state flowers of some the states where Walter lived. As in the inspiration quilt, I used 3-D techniques for the flowers, which are more folk art than botanically correct. I used no fusibles or other modern materials.

Though I usually prefer brighter colors, I really enjoyed working with Civil War reproduction fabrics. I did not try to match the fabrics in the inspiration quilt, but just chose ones that I liked from the Civil War time period. I have a new appreciation for brown, and for the women who made quilts 150 years ago using fabrics of that limited but interesting color palette.

During my research for this quilt I discovered my third cousins – sisters who, like me, are great-granddaughters of Walter. One is a quilter; the other is the family genealogist!

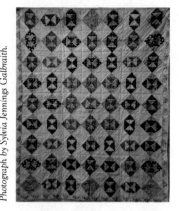

Broken Baby Dishes II
34" x 43"

Sylvia Jennings Galbraith
Temecula, California

The quilt I have chosen to replicate is a child's quilt made around 1850. I was drawn to this quilt for a couple of reasons. I liked that it is a true child's quilt (not a cut-down), which I could replicate in full size for this study. I was also enticed by the opportunity of closely matching the original fabrics, thanks to the many reproduction fabrics available to us these days. This quilt has the ubiquitous double pinks, so popular in quilts of the time, as well as green ground prints ("poison greens"), chrome oranges, madder and Turkey reds, and browns. It certainly was a blessing to be able to work with the original quilt directly in front of me.

The most interesting design element of this quilt is the layout of the colors. Although at first it may appear to be a scrappy quilt, there is a very intentional pattern created by where the maker chose to put her blocks. Note that the center is a set of nine pink and green blocks. These are surrounded by repeated patterns of the other blocks. Not all of the blocks are repeated, but most are. The three-sided border leaves no doubt as to the proper orientation of the design.

As I was making this quilt, I often thought of the paradox of a child's quilt in the context of the Civil War. On one hand, the quilt is a symbol of love, warmth, and hope, while the war was so very divisive and horrific. Was it made by an expectant mother for her as yet unborn child, or perhaps made after the child was born? Did the child live a long life? How did the war affect the child and his or her family?

The original quilt was used, yet valued enough to be saved for all these years. While we don't know the origin of the child's quilt, it's highly likely that the family was, in some way, directly affected by the American Civil War. To what extent, we will never know. I like to think of this quilt as a symbol of innocence lost.

Shield and Stars Potholder Quilt

41" x 51"

Pamela Weeks
Durham, New Hampshire

In the study of potholder quilts we have discovered a significant number made in the mid-nineteenth century in the Casco Bay area of Maine. I have replicated blocks from many, and decided to copy the center of this one, made in Portland, Maine. It is a Civil War soldier's quilt attributed to Cornelia M. Dow, the daughter of General Neal Dow, a national temperance leader and celebrated Union officer. Neal Dow is known as the "Father of Temperance," and devoted his time, wealth, and influence to this cause. While serving as mayor of Portland in 1850, he enacted the first temperance ordinances to pass in any American city.

Cornelia never married, and lived in her father's stately home on Congress Street in Portland, managing the household after her mother's death. Cornelia served on the executive committees of both the Maine Women's Christian Temperance Union (WCTU) and the national organization. The house still stands and is preserved as a museum, open to the public.

The purpose for which the quilt was made is unclear — its measurements are 71 x 81 inches, much wider than the 48 inches recommended by the U. S. Sanitary Commission for soldiers' cot quilts. It contains 66 appliquéd red or blue 8-inch star blocks, bound in off-white twill tape, surrounding a large center block depicting a Union shield. Each block contains four or five inscriptions, and the center block includes both inscriptions and line drawings. The inscriptions are especially patriotic in nature, all anti-slavery and pro-Union. There are inked depictions of flags, eagles, rifles, anchors, and banners. Cornelia Dow made several blocks, and these are placed in prominent positions near the center of the quilt.

Unlike most other potholder quilts, it is bound with woven tape, not straight grain single-layer cotton strips. I was able to use a running stitch to attach the woven tape binding to the front and the back of the block in one step.

I wanted to duplicate the central portion of the quilt in order to understand how to create a pattern for the Union Shield, found on many mid-nineteenth century quilts. I enjoy calligraphy and particularly enjoyed working on the blocks in this quilt, attempting to imitate several handwriting styles, including that of Cornelia Dow.

Oh Shenandoah
49" x 41"

Carol Born
Longmont, Colorado

Whig's Defeat quilts were typically made in the South, as was the case for my inspiration quilt. The quilt's owners, Jeffrey and Beverley Evans, attribute this circa 1855 crib quilt to Mary M. Trimble, who lived in the Shenandoah Valley of Virginia. This pattern became popular in the 1830s, when Andrew Jackson was elected President of the United States, and remained so until 1865. Jackson hailed from the South and was supported by those who wanted to protect their interests in slavery and states' rights. Whigs, on the other hand, opposed those views.

My reasons for choosing this quilt to study were: (1) The rounded corners of the center of the block were different than the straight edges I had seen on other Whig's Defeat quilts; and (2) I liked the outer border treatment, as well as the combination of piecing and appliqué.

In 2013 my dear friend Lorie Stubbs and I flew to Virginia to see the original quilt. We observed that the six "fingers" were pieced into the quilt, not appliquéd on, as I had anticipated. Why would the quilt maker do it this way? It seemed like a more difficult approach. We thought it reflected that the quilt maker was inexperienced and/or didn't know how to or like to appliqué. We passed it off as a fluke.

A few months later, while visiting Gaye Ingram in Louisiana, Lorie and I saw her collection of Whig's Defeat quilts. Sure enough, on the ones made in the mid-1800s, the "fingers" were pieced in, not appliquéd on, just like in my inspiration quilt. We were very surprised! Gaye confirmed that piecing in the "fingers" was the typical technique used at that time. I, however, chose to appliqué the "fingers" onto my quilt.

In looking at numerous Whig's Defeat quilts, I noted differences in the way the arcs were constructed. While the number of diamonds in each arc varied from five to seven, others, like my inspiration quilt, had a half-diamond on the end of each arc. I included the half-diamonds in my quilt. However, rather than hand piecing the arcs, I constructed mine using foundation paper piecing. I used silk thread to machine quilt my quilt.

A Quilt For James
31" x 31"

Florence McConnell
Manteca, California

Several years before the start of the Civil War, Adaline Frost of Southington, Connecticut, made two crib quilts featuring the Star of Bethlehem — one for son James W. born in 1856 and one for son Lewis E. born in 1858. These crib quilts were among nine family quilts donated to the New England Quilt Museum by Jack Reese, the great-grandson of Adaline and Lewis H. Frost.

I chose James' crib quilt for my inspiration quilt because I loved the visual impact created by the center star with whirling fylfots and the peony flowers in the setting pieces. This crib quilt also provided me with the challenge of my first appliqué work and the opportunity to learn more about the family. I was delighted when

another participant selected Lewis' crib quilt as her inspiration quilt so that the quilts would be exhibited together. We have had great fun researching and sharing information about the quilts and their families.

Adaline Frost must have been an accomplished quiltmaker and loving mother to make such an intricate and beautiful crib quilt for her son. The center star was perfectly pieced and the appliqué work finely done. In honor of Adaline and her son James, I chose to reproduce James' crib quilt using 19th century reproduction fabric. I created a pattern and templates to duplicate the design and size of James' crib quilt and then constructed my study quilt without the use of a sewing machine. I was able to obtain a detailed sketch of the hand quilting so that I could duplicate the quilting design as well.

I have to admit the appliqué process was more difficult than I had anticipated due to the small size of the pieces. The corner blocks and setting squares certainly looked larger in the photo than in reality. It would seem Adaline enjoyed the appliqué process, since she incorporated appliqué pieces into the crib quilt she made for her next son.

Apparently Adaline also instilled a love of quilts in her children as the crib quilts survived all these years in very good condition and remained with family members until donated to the New England Quilt Museum. This was a good reminder to pass the love and care of quilts to my family members so they may survive for future generations.

LeMoyne Star Quilt, circa 1860, courtesy of Colleen R. Hall-Patton. Photograph by Colleen Hall-Patton.

Red / Green / Orange / Purple LeMoyne Star
44" x 44"

Colleen R. Hall-Patton
Henderson, Nevada

Every time I describe the colors of this quilt, people make faces. Of course, when they see it, they change their minds. I bought the quilt in Santa Margarita, CA; the antique dealers had bought it in Ohio, but thought it had come from western Pennsylvania. I bought it because of the bold colors, but especially for the magnificent purple fabric. My experience with early aniline purple is that it fades if you look cross-eyed at it, so the homage quilt is a way to enjoy it without fear.

My version is scrappier than the original, but I also thought the lighter purple center squares reflected the one faded square in the original. All the LeMoyne Stars and partial stars are hand pieced, and I gained a new appreciation for the original quilter after setting in all those squares and triangles. I plan to avoid set in corners for awhile. This is my first quilt made with Civil War-era reproduction fabric, but it won't be my last.

65

Prince's Feather, 1856. Photograph by Denise Helms.

Feathers and Flower Pots
47" x 50"

Sandy Sutton
Seal Beach, California

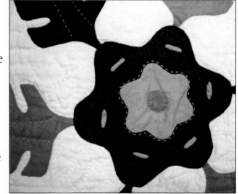

The year of 1856 must have been momentous for the quilter who created the wonderful red and green Prince's Feather quilt that I used for my inspiration. What important event led her to mark the year so boldly? Was this the year she was married, as suggested by the quilted heart motifs? It is rare to see dates documented like this on an antique quilt.

Solid-colored fabrics such as this are difficult to date. However, the "1856" emblazoned on this beauty led me to select this particular one to replicate. I also loved the appliqué border. This quilt is part of my Faded Beauties collection, as it is very worn and faded, with the Turkey red fabric abraded away in many areas. While the quilt's provenance is unknown, I am always pleased to commemorate the original quilt maker by copying or interpreting her design and work.

The Prince's Feather or Princess Feather is the most popular appliqué pattern in the four-block style, according to Carolyn Ducey, Curator of Collections at the International Quilt Study Center and Museum. The pattern is believed to represent the emblem of the Prince of Wales, which featured three tall feathers. However, recent research suggests the pattern may represent the red amaranth plant, which is also called Prince's Feather. Its first use in quilting is unknown.

To make the study quilt, I reduced the original patterns by 50%. While the original quilt is sewn by hand with the exception of the binding, I machine-sewed the blocks and borders together, as well as the binding. All the appliqué and quilting were done by hand.

My replica is not exact; I used six feathers instead of eight, and added a few more appliqué pieces to the vine. The quilting is also not as dense as in the original quilt. The red, green, and cheddar fabrics in the study quilt are close to the colors of the original. And I was not precise in replicating the appliqué and quilting motifs – flower designs, hearts, and feathers – to convey the folk art feel.

A love of mid-nineteenth century red and green appliqué quilts has led me to collect quite a few of them.

The color combination, most likely originating in the Pennsylvania German community, is very dramatic, and the style is quintessentially American.

The Fairer Flower
48" x 48"

Patricia D. Rennau
Fayston, Vermont

This is a tribute to Susan Prentis Prindle of Waitsfield, Vermont. I wanted to re-discover a quilt with deep roots in my community. I found Susan's quilt at the Vermont Historical Society. Given by Mr. and Mrs. William Walter, the acquisitions record notes "this is to be returned to Waitsfield if there is ever a museum there." Little is documented about Susan's life. She is footnoted simply as the wife of the Reverend Lyman Prindle.

Her quilt is constructed with a Combination Rose appliqué pattern. She meticulously completed 25 blocks and assembled them strip fashion with sashing on the diagonal. The rose design is a turkey red fabric on pink and white striped shirting with green leaves. The sashing and background are cotton muslin. In the 1850s, rose patterns held special significance for brides, and this color palette was often used for "best quilts." It is exquisitely hand quilted.

I chose to appliqué nine blocks, 9.5" by 9.5", assembled in the same fashion, set on point. Turkey red reproduction fabrics did not provide a convincing match. I settled on Judy Rothermel's Party of Five for "Turkey red," Chateau Chambray for the pink shirting and a Marcus Fabric green to reflect the intent of the maker. A maiden voyage, each step presented an exercise in trial and error, from calculating measurements, to learning a pre-turned method for the design, to mastering Liuxin Newman's approach on quilting stitches.

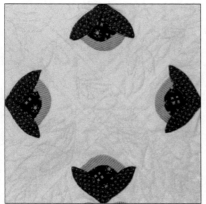

As I pieced together this quilt, hard earned stitch by stitch, I yearned to know Susan's thoughts as she created her keepsake, unmarried at the age of 28. Her father was a founding member of the Wesleyan Methodist Society in 1853. This society took a more radical position on slavery. Reverend Lyman Prindle served as pastor from 1853-1860, during the period Susan worked on this quilt. Susan would have participated in church activities such as the Maternal Association and Tract Society. Was she captivated by this charismatic preacher? Was there hope in her heart as she carefully placed each stitch?

In January 1882, at 57, she married Reverend Lyman Prindle, fifteen years her senior, after the death of his first wife in August 1881. Did she stoically assume the duties of a pastor's wife? Or at last find joyful purpose for her bridal quilt? Lyman died in 1888. It is my fervent wish that these six years together were the happiest of Susan's life.

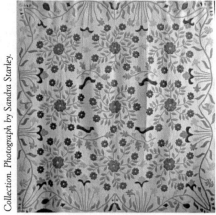

Quilted Joy Too
35" x 36"

Sandra Starley
Moab, Utah

When I discovered the antique Rose of Sharon or Whig Rose quilt, I was immediately enchanted and I christened it "Quilted Joy" as every busy inch exudes joyfulness and makes one smile. I love all the charming details: from the happy birds to the unique border. From that first moment, I wanted to recreate it and the Quilt Study was the perfect catalyst to get my fingers moving.

I began by studying the quilt closely and was very impressed with the design creativity and the amazing hand workmanship. The quilt appears to be a labor of love, going well beyond the average appliqué quilt. Rose patterns were often used for wedding quilts and it is easy to imagine a bride or her mother creating this joyous example for such an occasion. Rose of Sharon is a reference to the Bible verse, the Song of Solomon 2:1-3: "I am the Rose of Sharon, and the lily of the valleys. As the lily among thorns, so is my love among the daughters. As the apple tree among the trees of the wood, so is my beloved among the sons. I sat down under his shadow with great delight, and his fruit was sweet to my taste."

That blissful scene seems to come to life on the quilt with the birds enjoying berries while safely nestled between all the beautiful flowers.

However, our unknown maker could have been "voting with her needle" and used this pattern to show her strong support for the Whig party (Whig Rose) or alternatively, the Democrats (Whig's Defeat or Democratic Rose). Unfortunately, this quilt, like the majority of nineteenth century quilts, has little provenance and we can only wonder about the true motivation for creating such a masterpiece. Perhaps the maker was passionate about religion and politics or just loved to quilt like me.

I chose to make a slightly simpler, scaled down version. It was hard to leave out any of the wonderful motifs and the intertwined designs were a bit tricky to separate. And once the needle was finally in hand, the small scale made for many challenging hours of handwork (appliqué, embroidery, and quilting). The design process was continuous, as I worked to make the study quilt my own while honoring the vision and capturing the joy of the original maker.

Hearts and Hands
35" x 31"

Judith Thompson
Wenonah, New Jersey

This appliqué inspiration quilt is signed on the back in faded ink: "by Julia Fisk, NL Butt for Lt LA Butt, made 1863." It is a mystery if Lt. Butt was an officer for the Union or for the Confederacy. This hearts and hands quilt appears to have been a gift to Lt. LA Butt. Genealogy searches of Julia Fisk and Lt. LA Butt have been inconclusive. Some research leads to an officer from New York or an enlisted soldier from Indiana. No conclusion can be made without further research of the signatures.

The hearts and hands design is often observed on needlework of the early and mid-nineteeth century. Some quilts of this design have been made to commemorate marriage, engagement, or friendship. The design has medieval or Renaissance European origins.

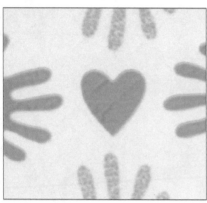

The inspiration hearts and hands quilt has 14" x 14" appliqué blocks alternating with plain blocks set on point. Most of the appliquéd hands are right hands; there are a few left hands. The strip pieced borders of pink, white, and green run off the sides. The binding is double pink fabric applied with rounded corners.

The fabrics are a white background and white backing. A pastel double pink calico print is used for some of the appliquéd hearts and hands. The solid green for the other appliqué pieces could be an over-dyed green. There is faded blue shadowing on a few green areas.

The quilting is stitched over the appliqué pieces. This quilting technique is seen in many appliqué quilts of the era. The quilting in white thread on the hearts and hands blocks is a grid of hanging diamonds. The white alternate blocks are heavily quilted in a feathered wreath pattern. Small circles are quilted to fill in corners. Perhaps the circles were drawn around a thread spool. The strip pieced borders are simply quilted in a 1" grid.

The center of the study quilt project includes one original size hearts and hands block. Partial feathered wreath blocks surround the center. The strip pieced borders are the same width as the borders on the 1863 quilt. Reproduction fabrics are very close in color and pattern to the original quilt. The quilting pattern was drawn off the original and is stitched in white thread, as is the original.

73

Rose of Sharon
48" x 48"

Pamela G. Koppleberger
Ithica, Michigan

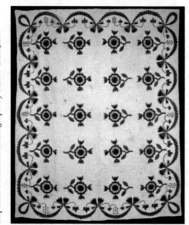

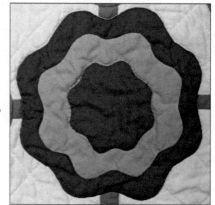

I am a self-taught quilter, first learning patchwork and appliqué techniques by reading quilt books, then by taking classes and studying quilts. I favor appliqué quilts, and the Rose of Sharon was the first appliqué pattern I made in 1981. It was raw edge appliqué, machine-stitched with a satin stitch on cotton / polyester solids. Needless to say, the quilt did not survive. I have learned various techniques since the early eighties to improve my patchwork and appliqué. I decided to revisit the Rose of Sharon pattern for my study and successfully create a quilt using my improved skills.

I browsed the Quilt Index for examples of this pattern, which has many variations. Some have a central stylized rose of layered petals with vines, leaves, and rosebuds radiating from the four sides. Asymmetrical patterns have a rose on a stem with multiple rosebuds radiating around it. Fabrics are typically solid colors of reds, pinks, and greens, with yellow and orange sometimes included. Many quilts incorporate a swag border.

My inspiration quilt is found in the permanent collection of the DAR Museum. The quilt has twenty blocks with asymmetrical roses facing the center of the quilt, surrounded by an elaborate swag border. I chose to recreate the pattern in a four block quilt with a simple border. I chose two shades of pink solid fabrics for the rose centers, whereas the inspiration quilt used red and pink. I used several different techniques to prepare the appliqué shapes, then hand-stitched them to the background. I finished the top with free-motion machine quilting.

I enjoyed reading the history of the inspiration quilt and the Rose of Sharon pattern. It has a biblical name, likely derived from a verse in Song of Songs, "I am the Rose of Sharon, and the lily of the valleys." Quilts of this pattern were popular in the mid-nineteenth century into the 1930's, often the pattern of choice for bridal quilts. Similar rose patterns include the Whig Rose, Kentucky Rose, Wild Prairie Rose, and Colonial Rose. In her book *Old Patchwork Quilts and the Women Who Made Them*, Ruth Finley states, "The best known appliqué pattern of all was 'The Rose of Sharon'."

The inspiration quilt was made in Missouri as a bridal quilt for Mary Ann Poindexter by her mother and sisters. She married Dr. John Marshall Staples on September 30, 1852. Unfortunately, he died during the Civil War.

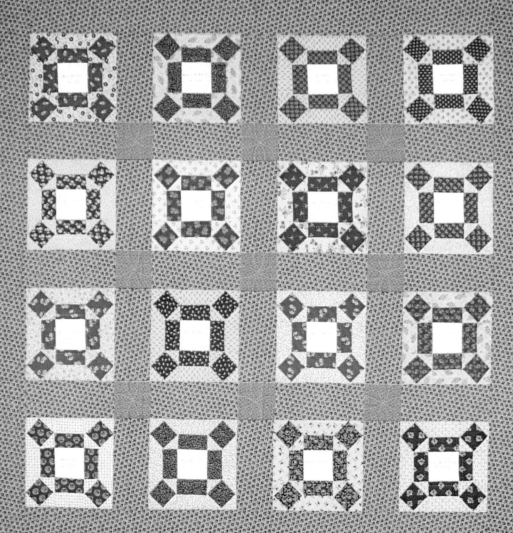

Honoring AQSG Presidents, 1980 - 2014
42" x 42"

Karen Dever and Didi Salvatierra
Moorestown, New Jersey

As Didi and I were searching for the right inspiration, I attended the Penn Dry Goods Market in May 2013 held at the Schwenkfelder Heritage Center in Pennsburg, Pennsylvania. One of the presentations I attended was by Nancy Ronk on "Fraktur Quilts." She had many samples of the style and spoke of a quilt that was from the Cinda Cawley collection that was now part of the International Quilt Study Center in Lincoln, Nebraska. Cinda Cawley was also our leader of Eastern Shore Quilt Study Group which we both attend. Eureka – a connection in many ways.

This fraktur-inscribed quilt (fraktur is a Germanic form of calligraphy) includes a block that identifies the owner and likely maker of the quilt as Aveline S. A. Stern. The block featuring her name also includes the German phrase "Ihr Teppic" or "her quilt," and the name of the professional calligrapher who penned this block, William Gross, inscribed at the base of a vase with drooping tulips, and the twenty additional names found on the quilt. This quilt inspired Cawley to begin a systematic study of fraktur quilts in which she identified the individuals whose names are found on the quilts and the relationship between them.

Cawley discovered that Aveline Stern was born on September 15, 1842 in Upper Saucon Township, Pennsylvania, one of seven children born to John Henry and Sarah Ziegenfuss. Aveline's parents, siblings, one nephew, and nearby neighbors are included on the quilt blocks. In 1860, Aveline was found in census records as a hotel servant. One year later she married Joseph Stern, who later served in the Union army. In 1867, at the young age of 24, Aveline died, most probably due to complications while giving birth to a son named Jonas.

Realizing that AQSG has been an organization since 1980 with several presidents over the years, we decided to honor their dedication and service with their names being placed on the quilt. What better way to honor Cinda!

77

Lyres and Laurel
34" x 34"

Terry Terrell
Masonville, Colorado

I selected the Sue Billmyer quilt (circa 1855) as my 2014 Quilt Study because I thought it was unusual and an extremely interesting transitional piece from the elegant Baltimore Album-style quilts to the red and green appliqué quilts. Sue's quilt looks much like a Baltimore Album block magnified to full bed size. The classically inspired lyre and laurel motifs were very common on album-style quilts at the height of their popularity. However, in the 1850-1860 time period there was a shift away from the Classical Revival style that was previously popular in architecture and home decoration.

I was especially attracted to the very balanced and symmetrical layout of the lyres and the laurel wreath on the surface of the quilt. The triple border framed and contained it nicely. I easily reduced and reproduced the appliquéd quilt top. The description of the original on the Quilt Index mentioned free-motion quilting. Some quilts from the time period had a variety of individual motifs quilted into the background but not connected together. Others had Greek key or

Baptist Fan quilting, both of which could be done as continuous line designs. The *West Virginia Quilts and Quilt Makers* book description hinted at something quite different.

I became curious about how the original was quilted and was able to track it down. I was stunned! The quilting on the original was a very artistic, mostly continuous line vine sprouting flowers, buds, leaves, tendrils, and fruit in great profusion and huge variety. Most appeared to have been influenced by early Tree of Life designs. Loops of ribbon were quilted into difficult areas where vines did not reach. Only the border with its feathered vine backed by a basket-like design was familiar. I had to simplify the original designs to fit into a surface area less than one tenth the size of the original, and to be feasible for machine quilting. Trying to reproduce Sue's exuberant, artistic, fanciful technique was the hardest quilting task I have ever tackled. It was the first time in my entire quilting career that I realized just how differently the original quilter and I approached our craft. Sue had to use both the artistic and the more structured side of her brain to design her quilt. From the exuberance of her quilting, I am convinced the quilting was as much fun for her as it was difficult and challenging for me.

The Mt. Ida Quilt Project: One Community, Two Quilts, Three Centuries

39" x 51"

The Mt. Ida Society

Lucy Barnett, Gina Bliss, Millie Chastain, Carolyn Hill, Del Peters, Anne Stapleton, Beth Weeks, Lou Boggs, Cindi Greene, Nancy Howle, Anne Picard, Deborah Waller, Sarah Wright

Talladega, Alabama

In 1851, twelve women of the Mt. Ida community created a floral album quilt as a wedding gift to a young bride and groom, each signing her square with her name and the name of her plantation home. For the 2014 Quilt Study, thirteen women who live on or near the same land as the original quiltmakers recreated the quilt, one-quarter of the original size, staying as true to the original as possible in construction and design, and recreating the sense of community that existed 163 years ago.

The Mt. Ida Quilt Project began with a visit to the Alabama Department of Archives and History to inspect and photograph the original quilt. The 28-inch squares bloomed with original designs of floral appliqué generously embellished with embroidery stitches of wool yarn and cotton thread. The same tiny prints and solid fabrics in vibrant colors were evident in all squares, resulting in a cohesive look. A six-inch floral-stripe border and clamshell quilting made this quilt a breathtaking inspiration.

Each twenty-first century woman adopted the square of the nineteenth century woman who lived closest to her present home. The artistic abilities of the original quilters varied from expert to novice, as did the skills of today's quilters. Working from photographs, a 12-inch template was created for each square. Analysis of the original quilt yielded a checklist of required patterns and solids, and a color palette created from paint chips guided the selection of appropriate fabrics. Working with designs that were significantly reduced in scale proved to be our greatest challenge.

We stitched and chatted at regular meetings in each others' homes, enjoying the same views of the countryside as the women who created the original quilt. We tutored each other, and as our needle-turn appliqué and embroidery skills improved, our friendships strengthened. We took "authentic" to the extreme by hand-picking cotton for batting from the Mt. Ida cotton fields, and by having a quilting bee on the site where the original quilt was finished.

The Mt. Ida Quilt Project accomplished its primary goal of recreating a quilt, but also created quite a buzz at the state and local level. It raised awareness of AQSG, spread knowledge of quilting and quilt history, provided the Department of Archives and History with valuable documentation, paid tribute to twelve forgotten women, kindled an interest in local history, and nurtured an old-fashioned sense of community.

Whig Rose Wedding Quilt
48" x 48"

Katha Kievit
Cincinnati, Ohio

My inspiration quilt is an 1861 Whig Rose red and green appliqué, which I own. The quilt has worn appliqués, but I liked the extensive quilting. One feature of interest is that the four "blocks" are circles. It was bought at an auction in Newark, Licking County, Ohio. I was thrilled to find two sets of initials and a date in the quilting: M.A., above M.D., above the date of Oct. 10, 1861.

My husband found a way to search and match the initials of two people with wedding dates in Ohio. I

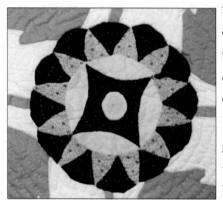

found Mary Jane Duff and Marcus Atkinson and the exact wedding date in Guernsey County, Ohio. This county is one county away from the auction site. I feel this is strong evidence for the match. One other clue is that a quilt on pages 36-37 of Ricky Clark's book, Quilted Gardens, is made by Eliza Jane Duff Stewart (1786-1878), Knox Township, Guernsey County, Ohio. She might possibly be a great-aunt or other relative of Mary Jane, and might be the maker of this quilt. Mary Jane, born in 1837, was 24 years old in 1861 and was living in Knox Township in 1880.

My approach to this quilt was to make one block with four borders. I used the quilt to copy all appliqués and quilting. I used my antique Turkey red, antique pink given to me by Xenia Cord, new yellow fabric, and sun-bleached green. The inner rose circle is pieced of 29 pieces (except the small circle), then appliquéd to the large white background circle. That circle is appliquéd to a white square with a hole cut out. This is appliquéd, not pieced, as I could see this in a torn place. I still do not know why she did this most difficult method, except by tradition.

The central circle is quilted in concentric circles ⅜" apart through the appliqués. However, the straight lines of the border are not quilted through the appliqués. There are two rows of double lines of circular feathers around the circle. There are corners of crosshatch ⅜" x ⅜" wide. All quilt lines are ⅜" wide. All quilting on the inspiration quilt is 11 to 12 stitches per inch, counted on one side. All the work on my study quilt is by hand.

I learned an interesting style of red / green appliqué that can be passed on to others looking for a regional style for dating quilts.

Stars and Flag Quilt
26" x 29"

Dawn Cook-Ronnigen
Broomfield, Colorado

My inspiration quilt was chosen because it had a patriotic theme for the 1850-1865 time period. By current judged quilt show standards it also has an unusual layout. The unique setting with the central flag appealed to me.

I was fortunate the owner of the quilt, Jeananne Wright, generously allowed me to borrow the treasured original. I took close up photographs of the quilt including each star, the flag, binding, and backing. On the photos I added observational notes on thread, fabric, and stitching.

In designing my reproduction I reduced the size to fit within the study guidelines and to have a wall size quilt. It was important to me that I use the same layout as the original and I incorporated what we might consider mistakes using today's aesthetic quilt standards. The layout includes omitted sashing, partial stars, and cut off star points. In executing the design I stitched the entire quilt by hand as the original maker did. I used 100% cotton fabric, batting, light, and dark thread to replicate the materials of the time.

The quilt's central flag design inspired me to research the use of flags in American history. The American flag was changing during the study period (1850-1865) with the split between the North and South as well as the admission of new states to the Union. Patriotism ran high during the Civil War.

Numerous military flags were used in the Civil War in both the North and the South. There were numerous flags for infantry, cavalry, and artillery regiments and battalions. The Navy also used multiple national flag styles. Brigades, divisions, and corps also carried designation flags. In some cases flags were homemade and presented to the military companies. Flags were protected by a color guard of a regiment's most experienced noncommissioned officers. A flag was also a rallying point in the confusion of battle.

Flags are enormously important in the history of our nation. Seeing the stars and stripes in any form evokes strong emotion and sentiment. The maker of the inspiration quilt identified with a particular flag design that was important to capture and preserve in a quilt. Imagine the anonymous maker's surprise if he / she could see it now.

85

Ohio Princess Feather
48" x 48"

Sharon Pinka
Bellville, Ohio

I selected my circa 1860 Princess Feather as my inspiration quilt for three reasons: one – fortunately, I already owned it; two – the fabric, batting, and backing had separated down the middle, needing extensive repair, so I wanted to replicate it in some form; and, three – I was initially told by the seller that the quilt was created in my home state of Ohio, so I wanted to confirm that fact through further study.

By researching the name of C. E. Winters (embroidered in cross-stitch on the quilt), I was able to identify the maker as Cynthia Ellen Winters. Cynthia was born in 1842 in rural Clark County, Ohio. In 1863, she married William Henry Harrison Sterrett, a local farmer who also served as a soldier in the Union Army. The use of her maiden name on the quilt indicates Cynthia made the quilt prior to her marriage, dating her quilt to our study period of 1850-1865.

Cynthia's Princess Feather quilt is a typical pre-Civil War four-block style Ohio quilt. Each block contains an eight-pointed Lemoyne Star featuring one feather coming off each point of the star, surrounded by a large amount of open space. The colors are solid over-dyed blue / green teal and walnut brown. The ground is white cotton, with cotton batting, muslin backing, and ½ inch walnut brown binding. The appliqué feathers are quite primitive, with no two feathers exactly alike, indicating a hand-cut template. In making the new quilt, I tried to keep the same primitive style as Cynthia, but used period prints instead for the feathers, eight-point stars, and binding. Cynthia needle-turned her large appliquéd stars and feathers, but I chose to blanket-stitch the much smaller pieces of my Ohio Princess Feather blocks. When possible, I tried to duplicate the double-rod, feathered wreaths, and cable motifs of the original quilting.

While working on the study quilt, I learned that there are many different styles of the Princess Feather and that the length, angle, and "motion" of the feathers can vary. Cynthia created her Princess Feather quilt using a very simplistic, graphic style, and her choice of teal and walnut colors make the feathers very distinctive. Her feathers are set like the spokes of a wagon wheel. I chose to add more movement to my feathers for a pinwheel effect. By using Cynthia Winters' quilt as my inspiration, I hope to honor her creation and convey an equal sense of vibrancy in my own interpretation over 150 years later.

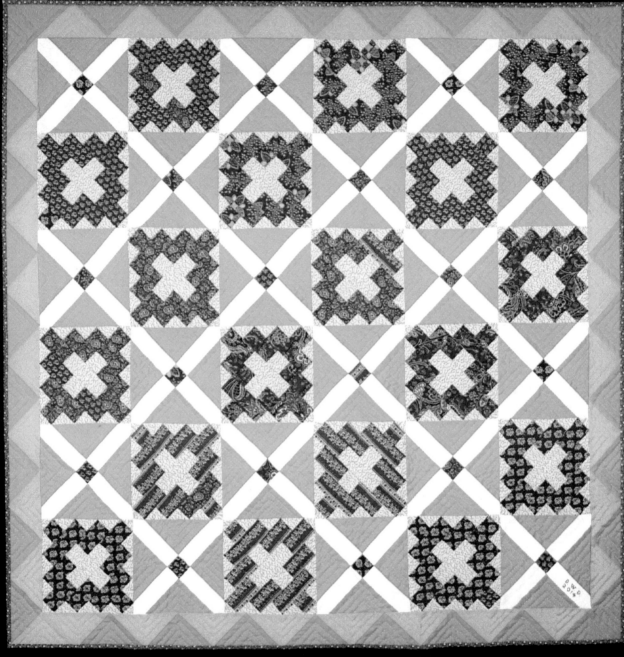

A Quilt For Susanna
41" x 41"

Dale Drake
Martinsville, Indiana

My Civil War-era study quilt is a tribute to all mothers who have seen their sons off to war. My great-great-grandmother, Susanna Frock Wentz, was one. Born in 1818 in Frederick County, Maryland, she married Elder Wentz of York County, Pennsylvania around 1835, and over the next 27 years bore fourteen children. Two of her sons served in the Union Army.

For this project I needed a Pennsylvania German inspiration quilt. One of the quilts in Pat and Arlan Christ's collection was perfect, inscribed with the initials of the maker, L.A.M., and the date, 1859. Thank you, Pat and Arlan!

Pennsylvania German quilts are known for their bright colors — white is rarely used. This quilt combined many red prints with yellow, green, and a bright orange border. I loved working with the red and yellow prints, but struggled over the orange. Be faithful to the original, or use a more yellowish orange that coordinated better to my eye? The quilt won out. Would Susanna have chosen these colors? I think she would have.

The album blocks in this quilt were commonly used in name-inscribed quilts during this time period. It was a time of migration, and my Wentz family was no exception: they moved from Pennsylvania to Ohio to Illinois and back to Ohio between 1850 and 1865. Susanna might have received an album quilt like this, with names of family members on it for remembrance.

I gave my quilt maker a name, Lydia Ann, as I worked. Her border had a corner resolution problem, so when I ran out of green triangles I followed her lead and used what I had on hand. I added my initials and the date in counted cross stitch just as she did, using an alphabet from a sampler and a strong magnifying glass – how did Lydia Ann manage without one? Finally, my quilting patterns were drawn freehand, spacing by eye as she did.

As I worked on my quilt I thought about Susanna. Did she make quilts for her sons' safe return, as I did for my son while he was in Operation Desert Storm? And what did Lydia Ann experience during the war? Did this quilt comfort her during those hard times? I thoroughly enjoyed making this quilt, which connected me with Lydia Ann and with Susanna, my Pennsylvania German ancestor.

Apple Pie Ridge Star, circa 1862. Collection of Constance R. Thomas. Photograph courtesy of Constance R. Thomas.

Getting to Know You
40" x 41"

Nancy L. Losee
Williamsburg, Virginia

During a 2008 visit to the Virginia Quilt Museum, I saw an Apple Pie Ridge Star crib quilt on display. I imagined the life of a quilter during the terrible Civil War. Even months later I thought of the quilt, and wondered about its history. The museum verified the fabric as being 1850-1865 vintage.

With the 2014 AQSG Quilt Study focused on this period, I was inspired to recreate my entry: "Getting to Know You." The gracious New York quilt owner sent me a photo, the measurements, and the name of her father who recalled he used it as a young child. Graph paper allowed me to develop the pattern to the quilt's exact size. As I worked a question stayed in my thought: Who might the quilter be? Where would the quilter have lived? As a genealogist I was able to find family members in Maryland as early as 1824 and some who lived in areas affected by the Civil War.

My fabric was ready to be cut, the paper patterns were laid on the graph paper as a final check and the design compared to the photo of the inspiration quilt. Check twice! Cut once! It was then I discovered the humor of the quilter. There are two patterns with outer curves reaching upward. There are three patterns with outer curves turned downward and one pattern cut in half and reversed. That was when I decided to call the quilt "Getting To Know You."

I do want to recognize Mary Robare, AQSG member, author, historian, and researcher. She was instrumental in assisting me in contacting the owner of the inspiration quilt. Her book *Quilts & Quaker Heritage* was most helpful in identifying quilting ancestors, any one of whom might have created the crib quilt. Quoting Mary: "Apple Pie Ridge Star was attributed to the blocks in that pattern on another 1858 quilt. In all fairness, the makers of the 1858 (crib) quilt probably mingled with the maker of the youth quilt at Quaker Meetings, since they were all under care of Baltimore Yearly Meetings."

The fascinating appliqué design and intriguing name inspired me to replicate the original quilt. With each stitch I felt a strong connection to the original quilter, wondering if it was she who encouraged my progress.

91

The Emily Munroe Quilt, circa 1865. Collection of the New England Quilt Museum, 2000.02; Gift of Hope Carter Ayers. Photograph by David Stansbury.

Emily At Home
27" x 45"

Judy Breneman
Green Valley, Arizona

A while back, I fell in love with doing wool appliqué, so I was thrilled to find that Froncie Quinn of Hoopla Quilts had published a pattern for the Emily Munroe Quilt. That made it possible to combine my new hobby with my love of quilt history. The Munroe quilt enchanted me with its delightfully folksy figures and its story indicating it was likely made by Emily Munroe while her brothers were at war.

I replicated fifteen blocks although I made a few changes in stitches and fabrics. I used Cherrywood hand-dyed cotton for the background as it has a soft look resembling wool. My appliqué was done in commercial felted wool while the original background and appliqué were done primarily with wool recycled from clothing and scraps that a rural family would have had. I also appliquéd two cats in place of dogs, simply because I love cats.

Constructing with the "hot pad" method was a unique experience for me. Each block was finished individually by turning the front fabric to the back to create a binding effect. At first, I struggled to make neat, mitered corners (feeling the quilt police looking over my shoulder). Then I learned that Emily had simply turned the wool edges to the back and casually whip-stitched them down to the backing, so I just finished the rest of mine *sans* perfect corners. The original backing was heavy fabric including ticking and denim, while in mine I used light cotton with a thin layer of batting inside. Finally I whip-stitched all the blocks together just as Emily had done.

This is the first quilt I've made all by hand. I love the results of the couching that was the dominant decorative stitching on the original quilt. Some blocks required 3-6 rows of couching done close together. It took me about a year and a half to appliqué just fifteen blocks. I wonder how long it took Emily to finish her fifty-four.

I thought often about Emily and what her life might have been like, especially as I appliquéd the house and the four horses. The horses may have represented her four brothers who were in the Civil War. I found interesting information about her family enclosed with the pattern as well as in the book, *Massachusetts Quilts: Our Common Wealth.*

A Soldier Comes Home
38" x 38"

Charlette Jokinen
Kawaskum, Wisconsin

During the United States Civil War, our soldiers wrote home to their wives and mothers asking for *spare* quilts to keep them warm at night. And, while in hostile surroundings, being wrapped in familiar sewn pieces of cloth brought them a little closer to home.

Many beautiful quilts are handed down through generations: each with a story of *how* and *where* their journey began. My inspiration quilt has no history attached to it; nor does it reveal its maker. Dated 1863, it is known only as *6832.9 Patchwork Quilt*. It is carefully preserved at the Minnesota Historical Society along with countless others.

I chose to replicate the Crosses and Losses design in the original; and while these four-patch blocks are simple and are not difficult, they do demand careful piecing. The center block of my project is an Iowa Rolling Star in recognition of the Seventeenth Regiment Iowa Volunteer Infantry, Company A. I selected the Baptist Fan Pattern for the hand quilting. This template was very popular during the Civil War. While I studied the original quilt I noticed a faded tract down its length and wondered why it was just on one side. It was then that I gave myself creative license and decided to give *6832.9* its own account of authenticity.

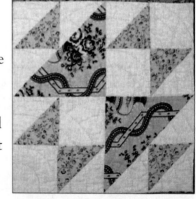

As I began to stitch my project the *how* and *where* for my trundle quilt came into focus and its journey is this:

I imagined a small room with a child's cot pressed against the wall; voile curtains playing on the breeze through an open window allowing the sun to shine on the quilt top creating the dimness of fabrics down its entirety. With my own permission I supposed that my third great-grandmother, Elizabeth Parker Guilliams, stitched this little coverlet for her son, Parker Willis, while her beloved husband Samuel was fighting with the Seventeenth Regiment Iowa Volunteer Infantry.

The United States Civil War was a desperate time in our country's history, and the heartache of the unknown fate of each precious soul weighed heavily on families, North and South alike. Although I am still a novice quilter, every tack of thread in my coverlet is lovingly dedicated to Samuel Elemas and Elizabeth Parker Guilliams, my third great-grandparents who sacrificed and endured.

Sue S. Jones Floral Appliqué
33" x 33"

Suzanne Brodnax
Eutaw, Alabama

The year 1853 was the relative calm before the storm. It was pre-war South – fabrics, designs, and time were available for some to make a spectacular quilt. In Williamson County, Sue S. Jones stitched her name and date into the floral appliqué quilt I have selected as my inspiration piece. Or did she? If only quilts could talk. The quilt reflects some financial resources, but there are only fragments of chintz strategically placed. Did a skilled slave stitch it at Sue's direction, or an older relative for her upcoming wedding to James H. Mallory? I don't know, but it doesn't diminish my interest.

I first saw this quilt at the Sam Davis Home quilt show in 2011. The Battle of Franklin Trust was sharing some of its collection including a recent acquisition, the Sue Jones quilt. The family had taken the quilt to a traveling television road show and were told it was of no great value, so they offered it to their local museum, Carnton (of the book *The Widow of the South* fame). When the family saw the quilt show, they were pleased. And so was everyone who now had a chance to see this amazing quilt.

I had already traced the quilt using vinyl overlays over a solid vinyl sheet for protection when the AQSG challenge was issued. My original intent was to make one reproduction for the museum and one for myself. The Battle of Franklin Trust kindly gave permission for mine to be the challenge quilt. And a challenge it has been!

First I selected blocks and a setting to represent its diversity, complexity, and charm. I invite you to visit Franklin, arrange to see the original – a photo does not begin to do it justice – and decide for yourself if I was successful. I reduced the tracings to fit the size guidelines. Then I selected the colors, matching

original colors when possible and guessing the original colors of the fugitive dyes from placement in blocks and likely possibilities from known examples and writings, using Barbara Brackman's books and series on colors. I tried to figure out how the rose petals were stitched. Next, I needed to learn trapunto. Sue's was not stuffed through the back, so mine is not either. I learned I cannot keep up with Miss Jones! But I did learn to stitch outside my comfort zone.

Wild War Geese
40" x 43"

Leah A. Zieber
Temecula, California

The significance of the red "X" appearing in the secondary design element of my Civil War study quilt is a mystery that I hope to solve one day. I am currently collecting and analyzing images of antique quilts that have this same design element in an effort to determine any significance or meaning. Like my inspiration quilt, most of the examples I have seen come from the northeastern vicinity of the United States. I hope to join forces one day with other quilt historians and share information so that we may form an agreeable hypothesis as to the design's meaning.

The original antique quilt comes from my own collection and is constructed of 182 Wild Geese blocks (Brackman 1692b) – with each block constructed from nine half-square triangles. In an effort to meet the size requirements for the study but maintain the integrity of the original quilt, I reduced the block by half. Given the small size of the block, I decided that a single half square triangle would best showcase the selection of reproduction fabrics I chose

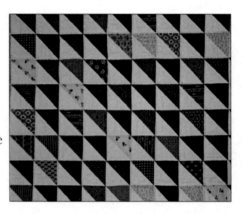

from my stash to create the quilt. This also allowed me to quilt the reproduction exactly as the antique quilting was done. The only difficulty I had while making my study quilt was finding fabrics that best represented those in the antique original. While today we have some of the best reproduction fabrics widely available, I find that we still fall short on many of the earlier colors and patterns that were popular in the first half of the nineteenth century.

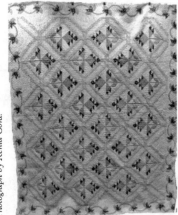

Kelius Oak Leaf
28" x 28"

Xenia Cord
Kokomo, Indiana

Searching for a study quilt from the Civil War era, I happened on an eBay offering from the estate of Judy Kelius (1943-2013), a long-time Pennsylvania quilt dealer and herself an eBay seller. The quilt appeared to be sadly eroded, and I wondered why it had found a home with Judy.

Once in my hands, the quilt showed its redeeming features: crisp red and green Oak Leaf blocks, dense quilting, and a delightfully quirky vining border. As I worked on my replica, I thought not only of the unknown quiltmaker, but of the previous owner, a woman with whom I shared an interest in quilt history. Judy was a generous and giving dealer, always providing extensive historical background on the quilts she offered for sale, recommending the blogs and websites of others for additional information, directing interested buyers to AQSG, The Quilt History List, and other sources of information to collectors and historians. Her previous ownership of my study quilt seemed to extend a personal connection begun through our occasional correspondence.

I followed the work ethic of the quiltmaker, constructing my small tribute entirely by hand, but I confess to using one non-traditional tool: to remove the tiny paper diamonds over which I pieced the red flowers in the border, I used needle-nosed pliers!

MONTANI SEMPER LIBERI

JUNE 20 1863

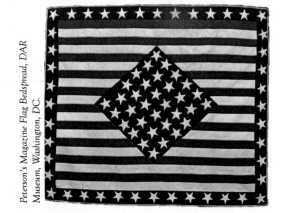

Peterson's Magazine Flag Bedspread, DAR Museum, Washington, DC.

Lincoln Steals Home
45" x 53"

Jane Crutchfield
Belchertown, Massachusetts

The graphic image of the inspiration quilt was perfectly suited to the idea of expressing the 'birth' of the state of West Virginia. The white stripes of the flag allowed me to include my family genealogy pertinent to the time period. I was born and raised on a farm in rural Roane County, West Virginia, so this quilt holds a special meaning for me. Plus it offered up the perfect opportunity to educate viewers that West Virginia is really a separate state and has not been part of Virginia for the last 151 years.

From the outset I knew I wanted to replace the center square with the shape of the state. As on the original quilt, there are 34 appliquéd stars representing the 34 states in the Union in 1861. The large background gold star represents West Virginia as the 35th state admitted to the Union (date on border). Blue and gold are West Virginia's colors. The state motto, 'Mountaineers are Always Free,' is located on the top and bottom borders.

I researched additional ancestors to represent all sides of my family. Six ancestors are represented (four Union and two Confederate). Included on the quilt are copies of handwritten letters from two different ancestors who fought for the Union. Additional family photos are also included.

I learned more about additional ancestors and the actual history of the state. After receiving permission from Shepherd University's George Tyler Moore Center for the Study of the Civil War, I included information from their website that further explains the role of West Virginia in the Civil War and its formation as a state. However, there is much more to the story than presented here, thus

the title "Lincoln Steals Home." In 1862 the constitutionality of Lincoln removing the "west" from the mother state of Virginia was a hotly debated question. West Virginia is the only state in the United States that was formed by a President signing it into law without permission from the originating state.

I always knew West Virginia was special. President Lincoln knew it, too.

Mrs. Pullen's Sunday School Stars

27" x 45"

Marti Phelps
Prince Frederick, Maryland

I was SO excited to find the topic "Quilts Made During the Civil War" for AQSG Study 2014!! I give quilt tours at the Smithsonian, and my favorite Civil War quilt lives there. It was created by Mrs. Gilbert Pullen's Sunday School Class in Augusta, Maine in 1863, to be used by Union soldiers in the hospitals in Washington City (now Washington, DC).

The original quilt does not have a Sanitary Commission stamp; however, it does have 3,675 words penned on it by Mrs. Pullen's teenage scholars (barely legible today). It can be studied in Virginia Eisemon's research paper in *Uncoverings* 2004, and in *Civil War Quilts*, written by Pam Weeks and Don Beld. The original quilt is called "The Sunday School Scholars Quilt."

I have recreated the 15 star blocks. Each block is pieced, quilted, and bound separately, and then the blocks are slip-stitched together (this technique is called a "potholder quilt"). I have photo-transferred my favorite words from the original quilt in the four corner squares of each block. Inscriptions include nonsense riddles, Bible verses, practical or health advice, patriotic sayings, and life philosophy written as advice to the soldier who would be convalescing under such a cot quilt.

Thank you, AQSG, for the opportunity to watch the words of teenage girls in abolitionist Maine in 1863 come alive on a reproduction Civil War quilt in 2014.

Red and Green Four-Block Quilt. Photograph by V. L. Mummert.

Wild Thing
37" x 45"

Virginia L. Mummert
Harrisburg, Pennsylvania

I bought my inspiration quilt in 2005. I was not particularly interested in appliqué quilts, or in red and green quilts. But as soon as I laid eyes on it, I knew I would buy it. When an appraiser told me that it is probably a unique pattern, I wanted to know more. Thus began a search of the internet, books, and other sources of information about these red and green, four-block quilts. I had no background information about my quilt's source or maker, other than it was "found in a bed and breakfast in Ohio." I discovered that many of these quilts were made in southern Ohio, western Pennsylvania, and what is now northern West Virginia. My reading told me that the design inspiration for my quilt was assuredly German, and that it was most likely made by a young woman, probably before her marriage.

I learned about the American Quilt Study Group's quilt study from one of Barbara Brackman's blogs. It seemed a perfect way to share my quilt with people who would appreciate it. What I didn't realize was how much I would learn by making this copy. Not just about the mechanics of making this kind of quilt, but about how we today differ from the way our quilting ancestors thought about design, about perfection, and about DOING.

Today, we are used to having the tools to do a thing "perfectly" (computers, copying machines, cameras). Letting go of perfection and just having "a go" at something can be downright paralyzing. But just because we *can* buy patterns, Mylar washers and spray starch, glue with a needle-nose applicator, stem-making rods, and wash-away adhesives, doesn't mean we *have* to always use these methods. I did make templates from the original quilt, but that was more because I wanted my copy to be as similar as possible to it. And I most certainly used my expensive, sharp scissors, my Ott lights, colored threads so my stitches would be invisible, and modern batting and fabrics.

Once the "perfection" hurdle was cleared, though, I found that going back to basics presented challenges and a unique learning experience. I found that even though these quilts' designs might look "primitive" to our eyes, there was nothing simple about creating them. These women knew what they were doing, both with a needle and with design.

The Chase Is On
45" x 45"

Vicki Hodge
Westville, Indiana

Scrap quilts are my favorite format. The eye is constantly moving across the quilt surface discovering treasures that the cursory observer passes by. Flying Geese are one of my favorite units – a pleasant reminder of the Midwest autumn. My inspiration quilt combines both of these. The unexpected border treatment was 'icing on the cake.'

I chose to reproduce the original quilt. I consider my quilt to be a product of three generations. The first generation is the original quiltmaker who created a masterpiece (to my eye) with rudimentary tools. The second generation is the era of my appliances – my mom's 1951 Singer sewing machine and GE steam iron. With Flying Geese this small, a good steam iron is a must. The third generation is the 'age of the internet.' The internet was instrumental in finding the quilt owner, searching for pink fabric to supplement my stash yardage (generously gifted by an internet acquaintance I've never met) and refreshing my memory on the Quilter's Knot via a YouTube video.

I embraced the scrap quilt format. All the fabrics in the quilt, with the exception of the wide muslin backing, were from stash – most pieces were leftover snippets from other projects. Each block was a fabric treasure hunt - my favorite aspect of quilting.

Close examination of each block leads me to question if the original quilt was pieced by two quiltmakers. The Flying Geese blocks in the lower section of the quilt show controlled symmetry of fabric placement by value. The upper section and borders are much freer in format. Each border is independent – the right border is high contrast with the inside row mainly plain muslin. No other border incorporates plain fabric. The top border is very low contrast. Reading the clues, I think the bottom border was pieced last, right to left, as there are two 'pieced' pieces near the left edge.

My piecing style is aligned with the 'controlled' lower section of the quilt. My eye is wired for symmetry. It was fun to 'go with the flow' in the interpretation of the upper section of the quilt.

The greatest 'take away' for me was the re-introduction to the joy of hand-quilting. As an adult we often abandon things that frustrate us – because we can. Walking away from my frustration wasn't an option. You can 'teach an old dog new tricks'!

Guidelines for the 2014 Quilt Study

The American Quilt Study Group invited members to create a reproduction quilt for the eighth biennial Quilt Study to be exhibited at the 2014 Seminar in Milwaukee, Wisconsin. The focus of the AQSG Quilt Study is to offer participants a way of learning about our quilt heritage and to promote AQSG.

The guidelines:

- For purposes of this Quilt Study a Civil War Quilt is defined as a quilt made between the years 1850-1865. The inspiration quilt must be clearly identifiable as a quilt from this time period using traditional methods of dating textiles.

- Participants may create an exact replica of the inspiration quilt, reproduce a portion of the inspiration quilt, or create a quilt 'inspired' by the inspiration quilt.

- **Only AQSG Members may participate on any individual or group project.** Each individual and / or group will be limited to submitting one quilt.

- An overall maximum measurement of 200 inches total for all four sides will be strictly enforced.

- To be considered a Quilt Study Participant each individual or group must submit a completed and signed Participant Release form to hold a place in the Seminar Exhibit. *This form MUST BE SENT VIA REGULAR MAIL AND MUST NOT BE POSTMARKED PRIOR TO JANUARY 2, 2013. Forms will be accepted as exhibit space allows through August 1, 2014.* A waiting list will be created when the 50 spaces available at the Seminar Exhibit have been filled.

- In addition to the Participant Permission form, a completed and signed Permission to Use Quilt Image or Photograph form; a digital image in .jpg format of the inspiration quilt; and a completed Written Statement Submission form that includes the written statement of 150-400 words regarding the project must be submitted to the Quilt Study Committee *no later than August 1, 2014.*

- *For a quilt to be considered for a planned travelling exhibit all items listed above must be submitted to the Quilt Study Committee no later than August 1, 2014.* Additional quilts will be accepted for the exhibit as late as the installation date of the exhibit at Seminar, but only if exhibit space is available.

- The Participant Release, Permission to Use Quilt Image or Photograph, and the Written Statement Submission forms should be obtained from the Quilt Study Committee.

- The photograph of the inspiration quilt must be in .jpg file format either as an email attachment or on a disk sent via regular mail. Scanned images are discouraged.

- A written statement containing 150-400 words must be submitted with a completed Written Statement Submission Form. The statement should indicate why the inspiration quilt was chosen and how it relates to the quilt study topic, what approach was taken in making the new quilt and what was learned through participation in this Quilt Study. The written statement must be provided as a Word-compatible document sent as an email attachment or on a disk sent through the regular mail.

- Incomplete projects will not be accepted. All submitted quilts must be finished (i.e., quilted and bound). All submitted quilts must also have a 4" sleeve attached, and a label(s) with participant's name and address and assigned Participant Number must be included in a bottom corner on the back of the quilt.

- Any quilt that does not fit within the guidelines of this study may not be considered for inclusion in the travelling exhibit.

Alphabetical Index of Participants

The American Quilt Study Group is believed to be the oldest and largest member organization dedicated to quilt-related studies in the world.

The American Quilt Study Group is a non-profit quilt research organization with over 1,000 members in the U.S. and abroad. Founded in 1980 in Mill Valley, California by Sally Garoutte with a small group gathered around Sally's kitchen table, AQSG has grown into a unique and highly respected international organization.

The American Quilt Study Group sets standards for quilt studies, and provides opportunities to increase knowledge about quilts and textiles, their history, and their place in society. AQSG members encompass all age groups and include quilters and non-quilters alike. Membership is comprised of traditional and contemporary quilt artists, quilt lovers, historians, researchers, collectors, dealers, folklorists, authors, museum curators, quilt appraisers, and students of women's studies.

If you are interested in quilts and quilting, their history and role in society; and you would like to help promote and preserve this traditional yet ever-changing art, join us!

Members of AQSG participate in the effort to preserve quilt heritage through our various publications, extensive research opportunities, yearly Seminar, and membership contacts. Your membership includes *Blanket Statements*, a quarterly newsletter; *Uncoverings*, an annual journal of the papers presented at our Seminar; research information; the opportunity to join our Yahoo Groups chat list, and the opportunity to attend our yearly Seminar.

Levels of Membership Support include:
$75 Friend
$65 Senior (65+)
$55 Student (full-time)
$120 Associate
$120 Corporation / Organization

Canada please add $5.50 for postage; all other countries please add $19 for postage.

American Quilt Study Group
1610 L Street
Lincoln, NE 68508

www.americanquiltstudygroup.org

Become a fan of American Quilt Study Group on Facebook

Made in the USA
Middletown, DE
30 November 2015